Sefer Yetzirah

Printed in the United States of America

First Printing: September 2017

ISBN 978-0-9842205-3-3

Published by Desert Mystery Publishing, LLC

Sefer Yetzirah:
Magic and Mysticism

Amy M. Wall

TABLE OF CONTENTS

LIST OF FIGURES

LIST OF TABLES

This book is respectfully dedicated to the scholars,
mystics and magicians who have kept the Sefer Yetzirah alive
throughout the ages.

Introduction

It is impossible to overstate the importance of the *Sefer Yetzirah* to the development of Kabbalah. The *Sefer Yetzirah* lies at the very heart of the way Kabbalah has been understood and practiced since the 2nd century. It also serves as the very foundation stone of the Western Mystery Tradition: much of what is now considered gospel by students of Tarot, magic and Kabbalah is derived from one or another particular translation or interpretation of the *Sefer Yetzirah*.

Despite these facts, the *Sefer Yetzirah* is a work often quoted but rarely studied by modern students. There are, I believe, five reasons for this. First, the *Sefer Yetzirah* presumes a fairly good grasp of Kabbalistic symbolism and is therefore usually well beyond the comprehension of the casual spiritual seeker. Second, it sits squarely on the border between rational thought and mystic awareness: students who expect a quaint textbook on ancient science are frustrated by its mystical language, while those who desire heart-filling, soul-lifting poetry are put off by the demands the text makes on their mental acuity. Third, the text places great importance on Hebrew letters. This is more than a little intimidating to people who don't read Hebrew. Fourth, the reputable translations available today approach the material in a pedantic, scholarly way that may be appealing to rabbis or Ph.D.s, but not to spiritual students; and it is true that approaching the material purely from the scholarly viewpoint often misses the mystical meaning of the text. And, finally, the *Sefer Yetzirah,* like most mystical texts, is written in an obscure mystical shorthand; intended solely for mystics from the same spiritual tradition, it indulges in no explanations or elaborations.

Even modern spiritual concepts are hard to express clearly; attempting to communicate very old spiritual ideas that have deliberately been rendered obscure poses tremendous difficulties. When we add the additional difficulties of translating the ancient Hebrew in which this work was written—with its lack of punctuation and verb tenses—we see that understanding the *Sefer Yetzirah* might seem like an almost impossible challenge, one that few modern students are willing or able to brave.

And it's a shame, because the *Sefer Yetzirah* has a great deal to offer. The time and energy required to decipher its secrets and penetrate its veils are well worth the effort. Jewish mysticism is the longest unbroken chain of mystic practice in the Western world. Long before the birth of Christ, Jewish mystics were chanting Hebrew letters and meditating on Kabbalistic symbols.

The spiritual worldview of the *Sefer Yetzirah* is fascinating. It is both complex—a five-dimensional universe consisting of many various manifestations—and simple—a universe of complete unity emanating entirely from the One Unnameable God. The lessons it teaches, and the understanding of the universe it provides, open new doors to dedicated students.

About *Sefer Yetzirah: Magic and Mysticism*

Sefer Yetzirah: Magic and Mysticism is not a work of scholarly interpretation or commentary: this feat has been accomplished by far more able scholars than myself. Nor is it an attempt to understand what the text might have meant to ancient Jewish mystics. The mind of ancient man is a closed book to us today.

My purpose is to approach the *Sefer Yetzirah* as a mystical/magical text with modern relevance. In treating the *Sefer Yetzirah* as a fresh and relevant spiritual document, I hope to open this work to those who are interested in the practices of mystical and magical Kabbalah, but who may possess neither the patience nor the interest to plow through dusty scholarly tomes in search of spiritual wisdom.

The *Sefer Yetzirah* traces the process of creation, the means by which one phase of manifestation becomes another phase. The *Sefer Yetzirah* is therefore of great interest to the mystic, who hopes to trace his way back up the chain to find God; to the magician, who hopes to mimic God's creative process for his own ends; and to the 21st century seeker of western spiritual wisdom, who hopes to find fresh spiritual insight in ancient teachings. This book, *Sefer Yetzirah: Magic and Mysticism* will guide your footsteps as you walk through the maze of the *Sefer Yetzirah* itself, and will help you penetrate the mysteries of Kabbalah's most fundamental work. Suggested exercises are provided throughout the book.

The particular Verses of the *Sefer Yetzirah* quoted in this book have been derived from my research and synthesis of the best available translations and studies of this ancient text:

> Irving Friedman's *The Book of Creation* (published 1977)
>
> Leonard Glotzer's *The Fundamentals of Jewish Mysticism: The Book of Creation and Its Commentaries* (published 1992)
>
> Rev. Dr. Isidor Kalisch's translation, originally published in 1887, reprinted in *Sepher Yetzirah: The Book of Creation* (2006)
>
> Aryeh Kaplan's *Sefer Yetzirah: The Book of Creation* (published 1997)
>
> Knut Stenring's translation, originally published in 1923, reprinted in *Sepher Yetzirah: The Book of Creation* (2006)
>
> Wynn Westcott's *Sepher Yetzirah: The Book of Formation and the 32 Paths of Wisdom* (originally published 1887)

The titles given to the Chapters and Verses are not part of the original text; I use these titles to help students focus on the essence of the Verses.

Judaism, Kabbalah, and the *Sefer Yetzirah*

The *Sefer Yetzirah* is unique in Jewish literature. It does not present the history of the Jewish people, nor does it reflect on morals or interpret law. It attempts, instead, to answer questions that concern us as much as they concerned our distant ancestors: Is there a God? What is our relationship to God? How was the universe created? In reading the *Sefer Yetzirah*, it seems at first that the text is only concerned with the second question, that of the creation of the universe; but, in a surprising twist at the end, we learn that the author answers the first question as well, revealing the Presence of God through the inherent structure of the universe. As the beautiful symmetry of the cobweb betrays the presence of the spider, so the symmetry and harmony of the universe reveals the One Presence.

Since the 6th century CE, mainstream Judaism has taken the form of rabbinic Judaism. Rabbinic Judaism encourages religious practice that takes the form of obeying Jewish Law as given in the written and oral Torahs and further interpreted by rabbinic procedures that have evolved over the centuries. Rabbinic Judaism is not a mystical practice; it is a way of living in the world.

Kabbalah, on the other hand, is the mystical practice of Judaism. Though the *Sefer Yetzirah* is possibly the oldest text in the Kabbalistic canon, not all Kabbalists study it. Kabbalah is a multi-faceted jewel, reflecting different faces to different viewers. To the Kabbalistic practitioner of traditional Judaism, Kabbalah is all about the mystical study of Jewish texts. The practitioner is expected to have decades of preparation in Hebrew, Torah, and Talmud before attempting to storm the citadel of the vast and complex Kabbalistic text called the *Zohar*, meaning "Radiance". The fundamental belief of this branch of Kabbalah is that there are four layers of meaning to biblical texts, and that the study of the deepest level reveals secret teachings to those who have prepared themselves to understand them. Meyer Waxman, in his *A History of Jewish Literature*, beautifully describes the impetus that lies behind such efforts. "Mysticism, like philosophy, arises from the elemental human desire to search and investigate both natural and spiritual phenomena, and to understand their manifestations more thoroughly. But, while philosophy relies mainly on human reason and accepts it as the standard, mysticism, which is permeated with the emotional religious feeling inherent in man, is, in addition to reason, actuated by revelation and inspiration. It is thus a third current in the history of human spiritual development, standing midway between dogmatic religion and philosophy. It is bound to rise in the life and literature of every religious people whose religion is revealed, and which revelation finds expression in sacred writings. These writings or scriptures in their literal meaning, can never satisfy the searching mind nor the thirsting spirit, who want both more of religious warmth and depth of meaning. Hence, bold religious people began to believe that there must be more in these writings than the literal meaning of the words convey, and that they undoubtedly contain some hidden mysteries, and therefore efforts are put forth to unfold these mysteries from the words of the Scriptures, to probe their depth and bring out the truths they contain."[1]

Less well-known are two other branches of Jewish Kabbalah: Prophetic and Magical Kabbalah. Prophetic Kabbalah is a mystical practice based on the concept that Hebrew letters and words, particularly names of God, have particular powers. Contemplating, writing or chanting Hebrew letters, words and names can elevate the practitioner's awareness to the level where he or she gains the "gift of prophecy", i.e., union with God.

Magical Kabbalah is related to Prophetic Kabbalah. Magical Kabbalah uses techniques similar to those used in Prophetic Kabbalah, but the goal of Magical Kabbalah is to alter events in the natural world. That said, though, the term "initiation" as used in Magical Kabbalah is often interpreted as union with God; so there may be more commonality between Magical and Prophetic Kabbalah than one might suppose. The *Sefer Yetzirah* is the primary source text for these two branches of Kabbalah. As a result, the

---

1   Waxman, Meyers. *A History of Jewish Literature, Vol. 1.* New York, NY: Thomas Yoseloff Publishing, 1960, p. 372.

mystic or the student of magic, whether from a Jewish or a non-Jewish background, is far more likely to be familiar with the *Sefer Yetzirah* than someone involved with mainstream Judaism.

The practices of Prophetic and Magical Kabbalah fell into disrepute during the Jewish Enlightenment of the 18th century. Fortunately, spiritual seekers in the non-Jewish world picked them up, dusted them off and incorporated them into their own work. It is fashionable today in Kabbalistic circles to speak with disdain of the esoteric orders of the 18th and 19th century which, having little knowledge of Hebrew and less of Judaism, nonetheless embraced Prophetic and Magical Kabbalah. Let us remember, however, that it was these esoteric orders that kept Kabbalistic practices alive (and available in English) until Judaism could return to claim them; the importance of their link in the chain of Kabbalistic history can hardly be overstated.

The *Sefer Yetzirah* is also of interest to modern scholars of Jewish mysticism, who study Prophetic and Magical Kabbalah in the same way an anthropologist might study a native tribe. These scholars do not practice the techniques of these Kabbalistic systems; nonetheless, their linguistic skills and historical knowledge add a great deal to our study.

Sefer Yetzirah History

The early history of this work is, quite simply, unknown. It is so old that its origins reach back into the realm of mystical tradition, rather than to recorded history. Mystical tradition often assigns authorship of writings such as this one to authors who are both highly regarded and safely dead. The *Sefer Yetzirah* has been attributed both to the biblical Abraham and to Rabbi Akiva (a revered rabbi of the late 1st and early 2nd centuries). This attribution, like those of all mystical texts, should be taken with a teaspoon of salt. We are unlikely to ever know who wrote the *Sefer Yetzirah*.

There is no agreement among scholars as to when the *Sefer Yetzirah* was written; estimates span the period from before the 1st century BCE all the way to the 9th century CE. For those unfamiliar with this dating system, please note that Judaism does not use the abbreviations BC and AD, which divide the history of the world into "Before Christ" and "Anno Domini," meaning "In the Year of Our Lord." Judaism, as well as most other non-Christian traditions, uses the abbreviations BCE (Before the Common Era) and CE (Common Era) to refer to these same time periods. The earliest reference to the *Sefer Yetzirah* is found in the Talmud (a central text of mainstream Judaism), which was completed around 600 C.E. The first commentary upon the *Sefer Yetzirah* was written in 931 C.E. by Rabbi Saadia ben Joseph, the founder of Judeo-Arabic literature and known for his work in Hebrew linguistics and Jewish philosophy.

The *Sefer Yetzirah* has been translated innumerable times into many different languages. Phineas Mordell, in his examination of the *Sefer Yetzirah* from the standpoint of Pythagorean number theory, comments that "There is hardly another book in Jewish literature, the Bible and the Talmud excepted, that has been so much commented upon as the *Sefer Yetzirah*. It has been the subject of deep study, not only to the mystic, who regarded it as the source of esoteric lore, but also to the philosopher and the Talmudist."[2]

Many ancient, crumbling copies of this work have found safe havens in repositories around the world, such as the Vatican Museum, the British Museum, the Bodleian Library at Oxford, and so on. A few of these volumes have been studied, translated and published, so what we have come to know is that each of them is slightly—or more than slightly—different from the others. Because the text of the *Sefer Yetzirah* was hand-copied, again and again, over a period of many centuries, and because some scribes evidently added their own ideas as they copied the text, no one really knows what the "original" *Sefer Yetzirah* looked like. Nevertheless, new scholarship and research techniques have allowed us to gain some understanding of the various "layers" that have been added to the document over time.

---

2 Moredell, Phineas. *The Origin of Letters and Numerals According to the Sefer Yetzirah*. New York: Samuel Weiser, Inc., 1975, p. 5.

Different Versions of *Sefer Yetzirah*

There are a number of well-known versions of this work. In order of their historic appearance, they are: the Saadia Version, the Short Version, the Long Version and the Gra Version. The earliest version was the Saadia version, which was the subject of Saadia Gaon's commentary in 931 CE. The next commentary, that of Rabbi Shabbatai Donnelo, was written on what is now called the Long Version, which contains about 2500 words. A decade later, Donash ibn Tamim produced a commentary on the Short Version, which contains 1300 words.

Fortunately for modern students, Rabbi Moshe Cordovero, a leading Kabbalist of the 16th century, assembled the different versions of the *Sefer Yetzirah* that were available at the time and selected one that best fit his understanding. This text was later refined by Rabbi Isaac Luria, generally believed to be the greatest Kabbalist who ever lived. This text was edited yet again by Rabbi Eliahu, Gaon of Vilna, in the 18th century. It is now called the Gra Version and is about 1800 words long.

Translations Available Today

Probably the most popular modern translation of and commentary on the *Sefer Yetzirah* is Aryeh Kaplan's *Sefer Yetzirah: The Book of Creation*, published in 1997. This is usually the "starting point" for students interested in the *Sefer Yetzirah*. However, despite Kaplan's laudatory efforts to make the text accessible, it is not an easy read. While this may be because Kaplan assumed his readers would possess a certain amount of Kabbalistic background, it often feels that Kaplan deliberately introduced a few conceptual "blinds" to confuse the uninitiated.

Another good contemporary translation and commentary is Leonard Glotzer's *The Fundamentals of Jewish Mysticism: The Book of Creation and Its Commentaries*, published in 1992. Glotzer's version is in many ways superior to Kaplan; unfortunately, Glotzer's frequent use of Lurianic concepts and terms proves confusing for students unfamiliar with Lurianic Kabbalah. Studying both Kaplan and Glotzer's work together, side-by-side, is an excellent exercise for the student.

In 2004, Peter Hayman published a pricey (well over $100) scholarly tome called: *Sefer Yesira: Edition, Translation and Text—Critical Commentary*. This version is intended for scholars of Jewish mysticism rather than the layperson or practicing mystic.

Translations by Rev. Dr. Isidor Kalisch (from 1877) and Knut Stenring (from 1923) were published together in 2006 as *Sepher Yetzirah: The Book of Creation*. The commentaries they provide don't begin to approach the level of understanding exhibited by Kaplan and Glotzer, and this book should not be used as a stand-alone text for mastering the *Sefer Yetzirah*. However, Stenring's rendition is noteworthy for the occult/hermetic viewpoint he provides.

Sefer Yetzirah Title

The words *Sefer Yetzirah* are generally translated as "Book of Creation." Glotzer comments that "In Hebrew, there are various synonyms for 'creation,' and '*yetzirah*' is one of them. Another one is '*briyah*.' An ancient tradition differentiates between the two synonyms. As discussed by Maimonides in his *Guide to the Perplexed*, '*briyah*' refers to the creation of being from nonbeing, while '*yetzirah*' connotes being arising from other being."[3] Through this linguistic analysis, we conclude that the author of the *Sefer Yetzirah* believed that creation came from God; God is the "First Cause."

It should also be noted that the word *yetzer* is often translated as "urge." For example, the Hebrew phrases *yetzer ha-tov* and *yetzer ha-ra* are usually translated as the "good urge" and "evil urge." So *Sefer Yetzirah* may also be translated as the Book of Urge, and the "urge" described in

---

3 Glotzer, Leonard. *The Fundamentals of Jewish Mysticism: The Book of Creation and Its Commentaries*. Northvale, NJ: Jason Aronson, Inc., 1992, p. xv.

the text is that of God. The universe comes about because of God's urge or drive to create.

Sefer Yetzirah Concepts

There are four concepts that underlie the *Sefer Yetzirah*.

1. God is the First Cause, the agency through which all else came into being. Even though God as the First Cause is the foundation upon which the book rests, it is also, in the end, the theory that the author attempts to prove. The proof of God's existence is, as we shall see, the underlying structure of the universe as demonstrated by the universality of the numbers 3, 7 and 12.

2. The universe was created by God through a process by which the energy symbolized by numbers and Hebrew letters moved from one phase of manifestation into another phase. The *Sefer Yetzirah* views creation as a chain that connects the One God to That which He has created. The Kabbalistic glyph called the Tree of Life envisions this chain as made up of ten links, or *Sephirot*. Today, we arrange the *Sephirot* in a particular pattern called the Tree of Life; however, this pattern is a fairly modern development, and it is unlikely that this pattern was in use at the time the *Sefer Yetzirah* was written. The *Sefer Yetzirah* is concerned only with the number of *Sephirot* (ten) and the number of connecting paths between them (twenty-two).

3. The universe is five-dimensional. It has three dimensions of space, one of time and one of spirituality. The letters and numbers create reality in each of these five dimensions.

Modern students have no difficulty with the concept of space, time and spirituality as dimensions. The *Sefer Yetzirah*, however, puts a unique spin on spirituality. This dimension manifests *specifically* in human life and in the human body. Kabbalah places tremendous importance on humankind.

Kabbalah refers to humanity as a whole as Adam Kadmon. Adam Kadmon is the microcosm of the macrocosm, a miniature of God. This view is not unique to Kabbalah. The Emerald Tablet or Smaragdine Table, part of the collection of Greek texts from the 2nd or 3rd century C.E. known as the Hermetica, says much the same thing: "Truly, without Deceit, certainly and absolutely—that which is Below corresponds to that which is Above, and that which is Above corresponds to that which is Below, in the accomplishment of the Miracle of One Thing. And just as all things have come from One, through the Mediation of One, so all things follow from this One Thing in the same way."

4. The most important numbers of creation are 1, 3, 7, 10 and 12. The numbers 1 and 10 are the numbers of God. The numbers 3, 7 and 12 represent the underlying structure of the universe.

The numbers 1 and 10 are, in many ways, viewed as the same number. Humans use base 10 for all mathematics, doubtless because we have ten fingers (or we have ten fingers because God's number is 10, depending on your viewpoint). All numbers may be seen as emanating from and returning to the number one, cycling over and over: when we get to 9, we start all over again with 1. In fact, according to an ancient Jewish numbering system called *Prat Katan*, zeroes are ignored; 1 = 10 = 100 = 1000, and so on. The number 1 symbolizes the One God: infinite, unknowable, unchangeable, first cause. The number 10 is the number of the *Sephirot* on the Tree of Life, which represents all Creation. And yet, since the number 10 is the same as 1, we see that the 10 *Sephirot* are the same as the One God, reflected on a lower level. What the *Sefer Yetzirah* urges us to remember is that God is both the number 1 and that which exists *behind* the number 1. God manifests the *Sephirot*, and to that extent He *is* the *Sephirot*, but He also has an existence that is separate from the *Sephirot*.

Another ancient work called *Sefer Rezial Hemelach* or "The Book of the Angel Rezial", the anonymous author teaches that "The ten numbers are nothing. Thus one and two, three and four, five and six, seven and eight, nine and ten. Then all calculations repeat."[4] What does it mean? When we add 1+2+3+4+5+6+7+8+9, we get 55. 5+5 = 10 and 1+0 = 0. Everything returns to 1. The idea here is not to prove the existence of God via arithmetic, but to see the numbers and the relationships between them as symbolic expressions of the way Creation operates.

The *Sefer Yetzirah* explores the numbers 3, 7 and 12 in great detail through the 22 Hebrew letters, which are divided into three categories of 3, 7 and 12 letters. There are three "mother" letters (*Aleph, Mem* and *Shin*), seven "double" letters (*Bet, Gimel, Dalet, Kaf, Peh, Resh, Tav*) and twelve "single" letters (*Heh, Vav, Zayin, Chet, Tet, Yud, Lamed, Nun, Samech, Ayin, Tzadi* and *Kuf*). Each of these numbers and categories of letters has a special role to play in the universe; each letter created something specific in the five dimensions of space, time and spirituality/humanity.

The Structure of the *Sefer Yetzirah*

The *Sefer Yetzirah* is divided into six chapters. Chapter 1 establishes the concept of creation proceeding from the employment of numbers and letters, and introduces the ten *Sephirot*. Chapter 2 discusses the Hebrew alphabet. Chapter 3 focuses entirely on the three "mother letters", Chapter 4 on the seven "double letters", and Chapter 5 on the twelve "single letters". Chapter 6 summarizes the earlier chapters.

The Tree of Life

One of the most important symbols of Kabbalah is the Tree of Life (Figure 1, **Tree of Life**). Before starting to work with the *Sefer Yetzirah*, it is helpful to have at least a small acquaintance with this symbol. Although the design of the Tree has changed over centuries, modern students will still find it helpful to relate the Verses of the *Sefer Yetzirah* to the Tree of Life as it is known today.

Diagrammatically, the Tree of Life consists of ten spheres, called *Sephirot* in

4 Sadow, Steve (trans.). *Book of the Angel Rezial*. San Francisco, CA: Weiser Books, 2006, p. 42.

Hebrew (*Sephirah* is the singular). The ten *Sephirot* represent different aspects of the structure of the universe. Kabbalah studies this structure by studying the characteristics of the various *Sephirot* and the relationships between them. The *Sephirot* may usefully be compared to archetypes of creation.

As seen in Figure 2, **Triangles, Pillars and Names**, the *Sephirot* are arranged in three triangles and three columns. Note that each triangle has a *Sephirah* on the right column, a *Sephirah* on the left column, and a *Sephirah* in the middle. The upper triangle, which points up, is often called the Supernal Triangle; it consists of *Keter* (Crown), *Chokmah* (Wisdom), and *Binah* (Understanding). The middle triangle, which points down, is called the Ethical Triangle; it consists of *Chesed* (Mercy), *Gevurah* (Severity) and *Tifaret* (Beauty). The lower triangle, which also points down, is called the Astral Triangle, it consists of *Netzach* (Glory), *Hod* (Splendor), and *Yesod* (Foundation). The last *Sephirah* in the middle column at the bottom of the Tree is called *Malkuth* (Kingdom) and is not part of any triangle.

The *Sephirot* on the right (*Chokmah, Chesed* and *Netzach*) form a vertical column called the Pillar of Mercy; it is also called the Pillar of Force or the Male Pillar. The *Sephirot* on the left (*Binah, Gevurah, Hod*) make up the Pillar of Severity, also called the Pillar of Form or the Female Pillar. The *Sephirot* in the middle (*Keter, Tifaret, Yesod* and *Malkuth*) form the Middle Pillar. Note that the words "male" and "female" are used in a symbolic sense and do not refer to gender. "Male" connotes aspects of creation that push outward; "female" describes those aspects that receive. The *Sephirot* that lie on the Pillar of Mercy typically represent concepts we think of as the warmer, kinder aspects of life; those on the Pillar of Severity are the harsher, more restrictive aspects. The *Sephirot* on the Middle Pillar represent aspects that balance warm and cold, expansive and restrictive.

As we descend the Tree, we move from beginnings and the desire to create (*Keter*) to endings and physical existence (*Malkuth*). All *Sephirot* between *Keter* and *Malkuth* are intermediate phases.

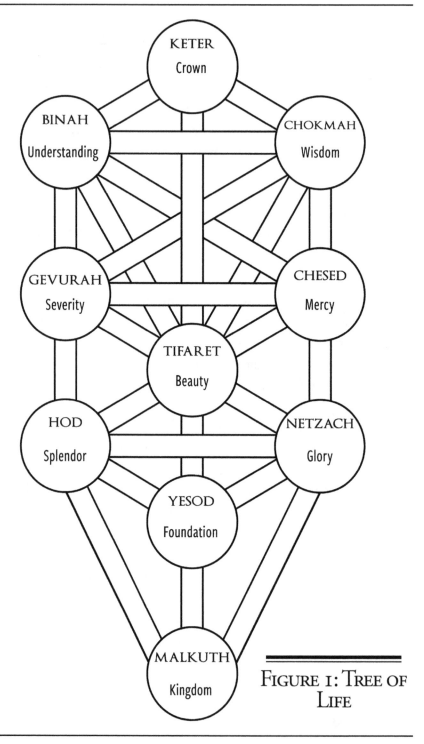

FIGURE 1: TREE OF LIFE

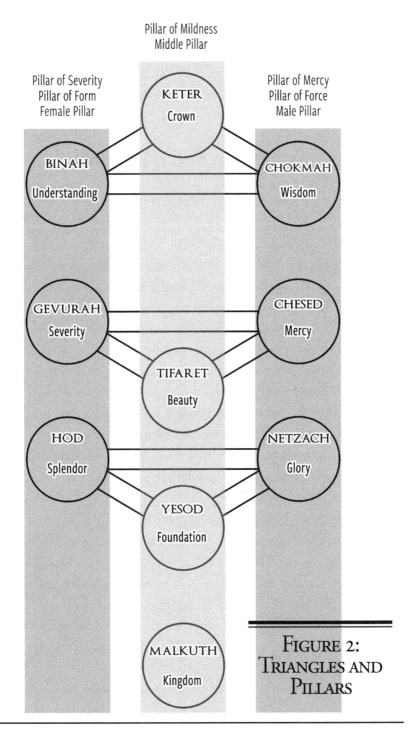

Pillar of Mildness
Middle Pillar

Pillar of Severity
Pillar of Form
Female Pillar

Pillar of Mercy
Pillar of Force
Male Pillar

KETER
Crown

BINAH
Understanding

CHOKMAH
Wisdom

GEVURAH
Severity

CHESED
Mercy

TIFARET
Beauty

HOD
Splendor

NETZACH
Glory

YESOD
Foundation

MALKUTH
Kingdom

FIGURE 2:
TRIANGLES AND
PILLARS

Twenty-two paths, which correspond to the twenty-two letters of the Hebrew alphabet, have been assigned to the paths that connect the *Sephirot*. As we shall see, the *Sefer Yetzirah* isn't entirely clear as to which letter corresponds to which path, so there is a certain amount of latitude available to the student.

Working with the *Sefer Yetzirah*

Using the *Sefer Yetzirah* for our own spiritual, meditative or magical practice requires us to take an approach that differs from that of the scholar: what students in past centuries believed is not what we believe; we may not be satisfied with answers that satisfied them. Kabbalah teaches that each generation stands at Sinai, meaning that revelation is an ongoing process. Though modern students should certainly study the works of our ancestors, this in itself is not enough for modern students. We must find God in ways that are meaningful to the concerns and understanding of our generation. To do this, we read our ancient texts and ask, "What does this Verse mean to me? How does this deepen my understanding of God and the universe?" As Allen Afterman says, "... the mind of each generation is in the next, the views of each generation are reconciled with the next; so that the ongoing revelation is never interrupted."[5] By making the *Sefer Yetzirah* relevant to us personally, we take it off the scholar's shelf, out of the museum case, and into our 21st century lives.

This isn't always easy. Kabbalah, like all mystic traditions, is difficult to understand. As Glotzer notes in *The Fundamentals of Jewish Mysticism*, "The obscure nature of Kabbalah is essential, rather than coincidental, to its existence. The difficulty in comprehending Kabbalah, the need to stretch the imagination as well as the intellect, are necessary elements in the generation of the mystic emotions—the marvel, longing and fear that are at the heart of the mystic experience. Yet obscurity in itself explains

5   Afterman, Allen. *Kabbalah and Consciousness*. Riverdale-on-Hudson, New York: Sheep Meadow Press, 1991, p. 46.

nothing. It is only on the border—where that which is known abuts the infinite unknown—that mysticism is born."[6] The *Sefer Yetzirah* lives on that border of the known and the infinite unknown. While we seek to understand the *Sefer Yetzirah's* text with our rational minds, we must recognize that another, possibly more significant understanding is occurring on a deeper, almost imperceptible level. Finding that deep place within ourselves, and allowing it to be nourished by our practice, is an important part of our work.

Sefer Yetzirah: Magic and Mysticism is designed to allow students to access the *Sefer Yetzirah* as it was intended: as a mystical text. After each Verse, you will find a discussion of the meaning of the Verse. While I will occasionally note an ancient belief or linguistic point of interest, my main focus is on what the Verse means to us as mystical or magical students. I then provide meditative and/or magical exercises; these exercises are suggestions based on my own experiences. As always, however, your mystical journey is uniquely your own, and it is best for you to work with the Verses in any way that feels right to you.

Unity and Separation

Unspoken, but clear in every Verse, is the co-existence of Oneness and separation. God is simultaneously one with—and separate from—His Creation. Everything emanates from God and so is One with Him; yet creation is an act of separation: dark is separated from light, earth from sea, man from divine, revealed from concealed, knowable from unknowable. If there is no separation, there is no creation. In this apparent conflict, Judaism aligns with the mystic eastern traditions. When the student perceives the simultaneous existence of Oneness and separation, then the mystic goal has been met, initiation has occurred, and wisdom has been attained.

---

6 Glotzer, Leonard. *The Fundamentals of Jewish Mysticism: The Book of Creation and Its Commentaries.* Northvale, NJ: Jason Aronson, Inc., 1992, p. 3.

Chapter One
The Ten *Sephirot* from Nothing

Chapter One introduces the thirty-two paths and the ten *Sephirot*, giving hints as to the nature of the *Sephirot* and how to work with and meditate on them. The emergence of the three elements and six directions, corresponding to the ten *Sephirot*, is described. The Chapter reveals the covenants made between man and God, which gave special power to human hands.

Verse 1:1 Thirty-Two Paths of Wisdom

In 32 paths of wisdom, did Yah, Lord of Hosts, God of Israel, Living God, King of the Universe, Almighty God, Merciful and Gracious, High and Exalted, Eternal, Whose Name is Holy, create the universe with three methods [Sepharim]: numbers, letters and their expression.

This Verse teaches us that the universe was created by the One God who is known by many names; He used 32 "paths" or tools in the creative process, as well as various means by which these tools may be employed. Ten of the 32 paths are the numbers one through ten, symbolized by the ten *Sephirot*. The remaining 22 paths are the twenty-two letters of the Hebrew language, symbolized by twenty-two paths that connect the ten *Sephirot*. Remember that the viewpoint of the *Sefer Yetzirah* is that

Hebrew is the language of reality—all other languages are translations of that reality.

This Verse also provides a long list of God's Names and attributes. This list differs from translation to translation, depending on which version of the *Sefer Yetzirah* the translator used, as well as the translator's preferences with regard to punctuation. Ancient Hebrew contains little punctuation and no capital letters, which gives translators a great deal of freedom. To give you some sense of how the perceived meaning of the *Sefer Yetzirah* can vary depending on version and translation, here are some of the available translations of God's Names.

> "... the God of Hosts, the Living God and King of the Universe, the Almighty God, Merciful and Gracious, High and Exalted, dwelling aloft eternally, Holy in His Name."
>
> —Glotzer[7]

> "Yah, the Lord of Hosts, the living God, King of the Universe, Omnipotent, All-kind and Merciful, Supreme and Extolled, who is Eternal, Sublime and Most-Holy ..."
>
> —Kalisch[8]

> "... Yah, the Lord of Hosts, the God of Israel, the living God, King of the universe, El Shaddai, Merciful and Gracious, High and Exalted, Dwelling in eternity, Whose name is Holy ..."
>
> —Kaplan[9]

---

7 Glotzer, Leonard R. *The Fundamentals of Jewish Mysticism: The Book of Creation and Its Commentaries.* Northvale, NJ: Jason Aronson, Inc., 1992, p. 3.

8 Kalisch, Rev. Dr. Isidor and Stenring, Knut. *Sepher Yetzirah: The Book of Creation.* San Diego, CA: The Book Tree, 2006, p. 14.

9 Kaplan, Aryeh. *Sefer Yetzirah: The Book of Creation.* York Beach, ME: Samuel Weiser, Inc., 1997, p. 5.

"...the Lord of Hosts, the God Israel, the Living Elohim, and King of the Universe, the Almighty, Merciful, and Gracious God; He is great and exalted and eternally dwelling in the Height, His name is holy, He is exalted and holy."

—Stenring[10]

"...Jah, Jehovah Tzabaoth, the God of Israel, the Elohim of the living, the King of ages, the merciful and gracious God, the exalted One, the Dweller in eternity, most high and holy..."

—Westcott[11]

The Hebrew Names of God are of great interest to all students of Kabbalah. Many Kabbalists chant or write Names of God as a meditative practice. Others use these Names to invoke magical power. Kaplan notes that, "In all Kabbalistic literature, it is taken for granted that Divine Names play an important role in attaining the mystical state."[12] Some Kabbalists believe that these actually *are* authentic Names of God; others believe that the power of these Names comes simply from centuries of use. A comparison of different Names of God assigned to the *Sephirot* by different translators and authors is given in the commentary for Verse 6:6, Table 7, **Single Letter Correspondences**.

Leonard Glotzer's translation of the first sentence of Verse 1:1 states that: "With thirty-two wondrous paths of wisdom, He engraved "Yah,"

---

10 Kalisch, Rev. Dr. Isidor and Stenring, Knut. *Sepher Yetzirah: The Book of Creation.* San Diego, CA: The Book Tree, 2006, p. 77.

11 Westcott, W. Wynn. *Sepher Yetzirah: The Book of Formation and the 32 Paths of Wisdom.* Kessinger Publishing's Rare Reprints, p. 15.

12 Kaplan, Aryeh. *Meditation and the Bible.* York Beach, ME: Samuel Weiser, Inc., 1988, p. 76.

"YaHoVaH," "Hosts," etc.[13] The implication here is that God engraved His Own Names in the world, so we may think of the world itself as being a Name of God, i.e., a description of God.

Sepharim, the word used in this Verse, has been translated as "books", "numerations" and "sounds". The word *Sepharim* may be the root of the word *Sephirot*, though some scholars believe *Sephirot* comes from *Sapir*, the Hebrew word for "sapphire," or from the Greek word *Sphaira*, meaning "sphere". Another possible source for the word *Sephirot* is the Hebrew word *mesaprim*, meaning "to tell", conveying the idea that the *Sephirot* "tell" us about God.

Verse 1:1 enumerates the three methods by which God created the universe, and they have variously been translated as "number, book and story," "number, text and communication," "number, letters and sounds," and "number, writing and speech." What is described here are three different ways by which information is communicated. In essence, God *downloaded* the universe—through numbers, letters and the means by which God used the numbers and letters in His creative process.

The *Sefer Yetzirah* regards numbers and letters as the raw materials of creation. Each letter and number is seen as a very specific energy that is directly responsible for creating a specific part of the universe. Modern students often think that the letters and numbers *symbolize* these creative energies; however, Kabbalah sees the relationship between letters and numbers and creation as much more direct: letters and numbers actually *are* the energies, not symbols of the energies.

Numbers and letters may be the raw materials of creation, but they cannot, by themselves, construct the world, any more than bricks and plasterboard can, by themselves, build a house. Bricks and plasterboard are useful only when employed in the actual building process. Similarly, numbers and letters are useful only when employed in the actual creative process; this creative process converts numbers and letters into the manifested universe. The various means of using numbers and letters—communication,

13 Glotzer, Leonard R. *The Fundamentals of Jewish Mysticism: The Book of Creation and Its Commentaries.* Northvale, NJ: Jason Aronson, Inc., 1992, p. 3.

sound, speech—are the building process. Thus, using numbers and letters, God speaks (or sings or tells) the world into being.

In terms of human experience, we can view numbers as left-brain expression and letters as right-brain expression; in this case, the communication referred to in this Verse would be the communication between these two halves of ourselves. Traditionally, the left brain is assigned to the left-hand pillar on the Tree, also called the Female Pillar, Pillar of Judgment or Pillar of Form. This is the pillar of structure, form, mathematics and intellect. The right brain is assigned to the right-hand pillar, also called the Male Pillar, Pillar of Mercy or Pillar of Force. This is the pillar of emotions, intuition and art. The third method, communication, could then be assigned to the Middle Pillar.

The word "vibration" would be a good alternative to "methods." The world we experience is one of constant vibration: everything is in motion, even when it appears to be at rest. Information is conveyed in vibration; letters and numbers are vibrations, and the means of communicating them is also a vibration. The vibration of the universe does not cease. Kabbalah teaches that God gives birth to the universe every moment of eternity: the universe is like a standing wave, dying and being reborn in every moment.

Suggestions for working with Verse 1:1

1. Speak the Verse aloud; then sit quietly, keeping the words in your mind. There is no need to memorize it; look at the text whenever you feel uncertain of the words.

2. Think about the concept that the universe can be expressed as the physical manifestation of the Names of God. Think about the ways in which this feels true to you. Note the exceptions that arise in your mind. What aspects of the world do not seem that they could possibly be expressions of the Names of God? Do not pass judgment on yourself or anyone else; simply note the exceptions that arise.

Verse 1:2 Twenty-Two Letters

Ten Sephirot of Nothing plus twenty-two letters: three mothers, seven doubles and twelve elementals.

This Verse provides more detailed information about creation. In Verse 1:1, we learned that the universe consists of numbers, letters and expression; here we learn that there are ten numbers and twenty-two letters, that the twenty-two letters are divided into three categories, and that there are three letters in the "mothers" category, seven letters in the "doubles" category and twelve letters in the "elemental" (also called "single") category. Later chapters reveal which particular letters fall into which categories.

It is important to note that this division of twenty-two into three, seven and twelve is reflected in the Tree itself, which has three horizontal paths, seven vertical paths and twelve diagonal paths. The assignment of paths to particular letters is one of the ways in which Jewish Kabbalah differs from non-Jewish Kabbalah. In Jewish Kabbalah, the mother letters are assigned to horizontal paths, the double letters to vertical paths, and elemental or single letters to diagonal paths. However, non-Jewish Kabbalists such as Eliphas Lévi and the members of the Hermetic Order of the Golden Dawn changed the assignment of letters and paths in order to make Tarot cards fit the Tree better. At that time, it was believed that Tarot cards were ancient teachings linked to Kabbalah. Today, we know that Tarot cards are a relatively modern invention from the 15th century, with no connection whatsoever to Kabbalah prior to Levi's time. While *The Sefer Yetzirah: Magic and Mysticism* uses an assignment of letters and paths that accords with traditional Kabbalistic teachings, an overview of the assignments that resulted from the linking of Tarot cards with Kabbalah is included at the back of the this book as Figure 20.

Beyond a more detailed explication of creation, there are subtle nuances in the diction of this Verse. The phrase "from Nothing" is used in Verses 1:1 through 1:9, indicating that the phrase is of some importance. The word for "Nothing" used here is *blimah*, which also means "not talking."

We may learn from this that the ten *Sephirot* were born in silence, exist in silence, and must therefore be discovered through silence. The silence referred to here is more than just the absence of conversation or noise. It is the absence of all sensory information, thoughts and feelings that keep our attention tied to the world of space, time and body. To interact with the *Sephirot* and learn the deep truths of the *Sefer Yetzirah*, we must enter into silence and darkness, distancing ourselves from the many distractions afforded by our senses and bodily awareness.

Suggestions for working with Verse 1:2

1. Speak the Verse aloud, then sit quietly. Consider *blimah*, silence. What keeps us from entering into the silence from which all deep truths emerge? Sometimes it is lack of opportunity: our lives are filled from the moment we open our eyes in the morning to the moment we close them at night. Sometimes it is our mind, running and chattering at us about fear and worry. Become aware of the obstacles that prevent you from entering and experiencing *blimah*.

2. Create a *blimah* experience. This is different from a pleasant meditation with candles and music; *blimah* is absolute silence. Find an hour when you can be alone and completely undisturbed. Turn off the lights and the various electronic devices that connect you to the outside world. Spend this hour going as deeply as possible into silence; feel what it is to be fully present with yourself without the distraction of sounds, sights and activity.

Verse 1:3 Covenant in the Center

Ten Sephirot from Nothing; ten fingers, five opposite five, with one covenant in the center: the word of the tongue and the circumcision of the flesh.

There are three concepts presented in this Verse. First, there is a relationship between the *Sephirot* and the fingers, i.e., the creative powers of God and of humankind. The ten *Sephirot* established in the previous Verse are now linked with our ten fingers. The idea that a link exists between something so huge and universal as the *Sephirot* and something as small and insignificant as our fingers is a crucial one. Kabbalah believes that humankind is a miniature version of God: we are the microcosm of the macrocosm.

As God creates via the *Sephirot*, so we create with our hands. Though the Verse does not specify which particular *Sephirah* should be identified with which finger, Kaplan suggests the following correspondence:[14]

	Left Hand	Right Hand
Thumb	*Binah*	*Keter*
Index	*Gevurah*	*Chokmah*
Middle	*Hod*	*Chesed*
Ring	*Yesod*	*Tifaret*
Pinkie	*Malkuth*	*Netzach*

As you can see by glancing again at Figure 2, **Triangles, Pillars and Names**, this configuration simply pairs the right hand with all the *Sephirot* of the Male Pillar plus *Keter* and *Tifaret* from the Middle Pillar, and the left hand with all the *Sephirot* of the Female Pillar plus *Yesod* and *Malkuth* from the Middle Pillar.

The second concept is that a creative energy is unleashed when parallel energies oppose each other; this is represented by the five fingers of one hand and the five fingers of the other hand. Just as all ten *Sephirot* are

---

14 Kaplan, Aryeh. *Sefer Yetzirah: The Book of Creation.* York Beach, ME: Samuel Weiser, Inc., 1997, p. 34.

required to create the cosmos, and just as the positive and negative poles of a battery cause electricity to flow between them, so we must employ both hands, right and left, positive and negative energies, male and female, good and bad, fire and water to create and channel creative energy. All the apparent opposites of our being can, by working together, cause creative energy to flow between them. Our intentional direction of the forces that come about through "five opposite five" brings power to such activities as the laying on of the hands, healing through touch, hands clasped in prayer, the Priestly Blessing, and, of course, magic.

On a personal level, we become more powerful in the world when we are able to access both our positive qualities and our shadow qualities. When we ignore or repress either of these, we lose our power.

Third, there is a covenant that encompasses words and flesh. A covenant is a bridge between human and Divine. The covenant referred to here, the bridge, is the ability to create. The covenant of the flesh refers to the ritual of circumcision, the ancient symbol of the link between God and Israel. Clearly, circumcision of the genitals is related to the creative process. The covenant of the tongue is the ability to create with language. The belief in the creative power of letters and words is fundamental to the *Sefer Yetzirah* cosmic view.

Suggestions for working with Verse 1:3

1. Speak the Verse aloud; then sit quietly. Notice that *Malkuth*, the *Sephirah* of physical manifestation and the Earth, is assigned to the left hand, along with *Sephirot* of restriction such as *Binah* and *Gevurah*. How does this feel? What arises for you in relation to this concept?

2. Sit quietly and consider your right hand. Imagine that all the goodness and beneficence of the universe can flow through this right hand and influence anything you touch. Spend some time with this idea and with the feelings it brings up in you. Now sit and consider your left hand. Imagine

that all the evil and destruction of the universe can flow through this left hand and influence anything you touch. Difficult as it may be, spend some time with the feelings this brings up in you. Now bring your two hands together, slowly, until they are about five inches apart. See if you can feel the energy and power that exists between these two hands. Resist the temptation to actually "do something" with the energies you've brought up; at this point, you are just noticing them. Then, move your hands away from each other slowly and let the energy dissipate.

Verse 1:4 Bring the Creator Back to His Base

Ten numbers from nothing; ten and not nine, ten and not eleven. Understand this wisdom and be wise in this understanding. Study and contemplate them, establish them clearly and bring the Creator back to His Base.

As was stated in the Introduction, the numbers one and ten may be regarded as the same number. One is the number of God; ten is the number of the *Sephirot*, the manifestation of God. In saying that there are ten numbers and not nine, ten and not eleven, the Verse is emphasizing the point that the *Sephirot* are a manifestation of God. In keeping with mainstream Judaism, the *Sefer Yetzirah* is adamant that despite the appearance of many gods, God is nonetheless One. The ability to find unity in diversity is a key concept in Kabbalistic teachings.

The sentence "Understand this wisdom and be wise in this understanding" links the second and third *Sephirot*. The name of the second *Sephirah*, *Chokmah*, is translated as Wisdom; the name of the third *Sephirah* is *Binah* or Understanding. The difference between wisdom and understanding is this: understanding is a state attained by the mind, while wisdom is attained by the soul. This Verse suggests that we approach the *Sephirot* with both our minds and our souls. Man is a thinking creature, and thinking about spirituality is part of the way we approach the Divine. But we must combine the work we do with our minds (understanding) and the work we do with our souls (wisdom) to truly contemplate the *Sephirot* and thus all of creation. Obviously, then, by combining *Binah* (Understanding) and *Chokmah* (Wisdom), we are combining the Pillars of Force and Form, upon which they reside. This practice creates a bridge between these different energies so that we may achieve balance.

The phrase "study and contemplate them [the *Sephirot*], examine them clearly" has been translated in various ways to emphasize the original author's intent. For example:

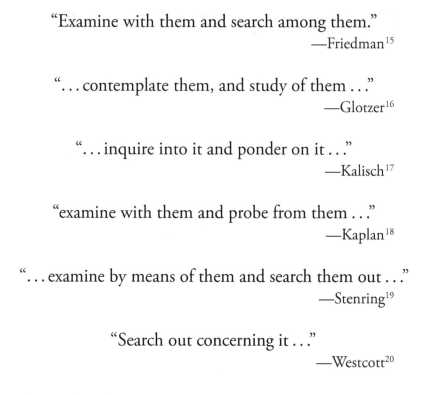

"Examine with them and search among them."
—Friedman[15]

"...contemplate them, and study of them..."
—Glotzer[16]

"...inquire into it and ponder on it..."
—Kalisch[17]

"examine with them and probe from them..."
—Kaplan[18]

"...examine by means of them and search them out..."
—Stenring[19]

"Search out concerning it..."
—Westcott[20]

But despite the differences in wording, we are being urged to regard the *Sephirot* with a deep and comprehensive study, employing both mental and contemplative techniques. The phrase "establish them clearly" indicates that we are to fix the *Sephirot* quite firmly in our minds, hearts and souls.

15 Friedman, Irving. *The Book of Creation*. New York, NY: Samuel Weiser, Inc., 1977, p. 1.

16 Glotzer, Leonard R. *The Fundamentals of Jewish Mysticism: The Book of Creation and Its Commentaries*. Northvale, NJ: Jason Aronson, Inc., 1992, p. 20.

17 Kalisch, Rev. Dr. Isidor and Stenring, Knut. *Sepher Yetzirah: The Book of Creation*. San Diego, CA: The Book Tree, 2006, p. 14.

18 Kaplan, Aryeh. *Sefer Yetzirah: The Book of Creation*. York Beach, ME: Samuel Weiser, Inc., 1997, p. 38.

19 Kalisch, Rev. Dr. Isidor and Stenring, Knut. *Sepher Yetzirah: The Book of Creation*. San Diego, CA: The Book Tree, 2006, p. 77.

20 Westcott, W. Wynn. *Sepher Yetzirah: The Book of Formation and the 32 Paths of Wisdom*. Kessinger Publishing's Rare Reprints. p. 14.

But to what end? The purpose of all this study and work is to "bring the Creator back to His Base." If we presume this Base to be *Malkuth*, the *Sephirah* of the physical world upon which the entire Tree rests, we are presented with a conundrum: are we asked to believe that the Creator is somehow not on His Base if we do not do these things? Obviously not: the point here is that by using our understanding and wisdom to study and contemplate the *Sephirot* we bring God into our lives; that is, into the world of humankind and physical manifestation.

Note here that the techniques recommended by the *Sefer Yetzirah* are entirely contemplative; there is no mention of the morality, laws, or tenets of righteous living that are the foundation of contemporary mainstream Jewish life.

Suggestions for working with Verse 1:4

1. We often wait for the Divine to make Its Presence known to us. However, the *Sefer Yetzirah* points out that is up to each of us to bring God into our lives, i.e., onto His Base. Realize that while mystical events may occasionally come to us unexpectedly and apparently uninvited, by and large the power to include or exclude the presence of the Divine rests in our hands.

2. Consider the difference between understanding and wisdom. What ways of working with the *Sephirot* help us understand them? What ways of working with the *Sephirot* bring us wisdom? While understanding comes through the mind, wisdom comes through the soul.

Verse 1:5 Ten Infinities

Ten Sephirot from nothing have ten infinities: depth of beginning and depth of end; depth of good and depth of ill; depth of above and depth of below; depth of east and depth of west; depth of north and depth of south. And the only Lord God rules over them all from His Holy Dwelling, for eternity.

The word used for "infinities" in the *Sefer Yetzirah* is *omek*, which can also be translated as abyss, vastness, depth, dimension or principle. The ten infinities listed in this Verse comprise the boundaries of the five dimensions of the *Sefer Yetzirah* universe. The infinities of beginning and end refer to the dimension of time. The infinities of good and ill refer to the dimension of spirit or morality. The infinities of above and below, east and west, north and south refer to the three dimensions of physical space. These five dimensions of space, time and spirit are referred to throughout the text, respectively, as Universe, Year and Humanity.

The *Sephirot* represent infinities, but they are limited infinities. The concept at first sounds paradoxical, but here is an example: there are an infinite number of positive numbers, and an infinite number of positive even numbers. Both sets of numbers are infinite, yet the set of positive even numbers is half the size of the set of positive numbers. Thus, we see that something can be both infinite and limited. Unlike the *Sephirot*, however, God is infinite and not limited. As this Verse reminds us, God rules over the five dimensions of the cosmos from His Holy Dwelling (also translated as seat or Throne) that is beyond all dimensions.

There are two Hebrew words for "rule"—one is *moshel* and the other is *melech*. Aryeh Kaplan explains that *moshel* suggests a dictatorship in which the ruler neither interacts with nor is influenced by His subjects, while *melech* suggests interaction between ruler and subjects.[21] The *Sefer Yetzirah* uses the word *moshel*. This view of God as distant from and essentially untouched by humankind is an unusual one in Judaism. Certainly, the

---

21 Kaplan, Aryeh. *Sefer Yetzirah: The Book of Creation.* York Beach, ME: Samuel Weiser, Inc., 1997, p. 50.

God of the Torah is deeply involved in human affairs. The Kabbalistic text *Zohar* informs us that "Whatever He does in heaven or intends to do in the world, He does by means of the righteous, hiding nothing from them. For the blessed Holy One desires to collaborate with the righteous, so that the wicked will have no pretext to complain about anything He does."[22] This suggests a strong interaction between ruler and subject.

But the God of the *Sefer Yetzirah* is not the God of the Torah or the *Zohar*; this God is a remote, removed Being who exists outside the five dimensions of human experience. He rules the universe absolutely and unconditionally, and is far beyond human comprehension.

The ten attributes or infinities listed in this Verse are assigned to the *Sephirot*, but there is no consensus as to their assignment. The dimension of time and our three physical dimensions can be assigned to the *Sephirot* more or less at random, but things get complex when considering the moral dimension. That which is "ill" is often assigned to *Malkuth*, in accordance with the generally held view that our physical universe, represented by *Malkuth*, is a place of evil. Alternately, ill may be assigned to *Gevurah*, the *Sephirah* of restriction, or *Binah*, the *Sephirah* of birth and death. Good is then assigned to *Keter* (as the "opposite" of *Malkuth*), *Chesed* (as the "opposite" of *Gevurah*) or *Chokmah* (as the "opposite" of *Binah*).

By including good and ill as dimensions of creation, the *Sefer Yetzirah* makes good and ill relative terms. When we ask if something in physical space is up, we are comparing it to another object in physical space. A balloon in the air is up compared to the person standing below it, but it is down compared to the bird flying overhead. If we ask a person if they live north or south of us, they cannot answer until they know exactly where we live. The same is true for time; an event occurs early or late when compared with another event. Similarly, then, what is good for one person may be ill for another. This notion of relative morality is very much at odds with the Torah, which removes any possibility of moral relativism by laying out very specific rules for Jews to follow. One way of reconciling this difficulty

---

22 Matt, Daniel. *The Zohar, Volume 2.* Stanford, CA: Stanford University Press, 2004, p. 139.

is an idea that approaches heresy: the Torah is intended for the general population, while the *Sefer Yetzirah* is intended for mystics. Since the Torah is regarded by mainstream Judaism as the literal word of God, the notion that there may be deeper teachings than those found in the Torah would indeed be heretical to the conventional practitioner of Judaism.

Many Kabbalists struggle with the idea that evil may have its origins in any of the *Sephirot*. This struggle has resulted in the creation of a number of Kabbalistic myths about shadow *Sephirot*, broken vessels, and so on. These ideas result entirely from an inability to reconcile what appears evil (from the limited human viewpoint) with the fantasy of a God who is entirely good. The apparent contradiction of a wholly good God with an evil universe is one that troubles people from all religious backgrounds; however, the *Sefer Yetzirah* states clearly that evil is an integral part of the design of our universe.

Suggestions for working Verse 1:5

1. Consider an event that feels evil to you. It's best to start with something fairly small on the evil scale, rather than something cataclysmic. For just a few minutes, think of this event as a matter of perspective rather than as evil; acknowledge that this event seems evil from your own viewpoint, but to someone else it may appear quite different.

2. Verse 1.5 is often used as a Kabbalistic meditation upon infinity. Consider, first, an infinity of beginning. Cast your mind far back in time, before your birth, before the founding of your country, before the written word, before humankind appeared on earth, before earth was created, before the sun was born. Keep going, further and further back, and recognize that no matter how long you sat and contemplated this, the beginning of time would be still further back. Now cast your mind forward to the end of time. Imagine the end of humankind, the inevitable death of our sun, the birth of new galaxies and their death, and recognize

that no matter how long you sat in this contemplation, the end of time would be still further out.

Use this contemplation for several days, considering a different pair of dimensions each day: above and below, east and west, north and south, good and ill. When contemplating physical dimensions, send your mind out into the physical universe in that direction as far as possible. No matter how far you imagine east, for example, there is still more of the universe in the east direction. When contemplating good and ill, remember that these are dimensions of morality. "Good" would be the best, most spiritual, most advanced, etc., creature that you could imagine. No matter how "good" a creature you imagine, there is yet more goodness possible. "Ill" would be the worst, most evil, selfish, violent creature you could imagine; but there is always more evil, more selfish and more violence possible.

The goal here is to recognize that God is larger than we can ever imagine. One of the crucial aspects of this contemplation is to realize that God is in evil as well as good, in the future as in the past, and in all directions. God is infinite: no matter how much time we spend contemplating these various dimensions, we can never truly wrap our minds around God.

Verse 1:6 Lightning Flash Without End

Ten Sephirot of Nothing have the appearance of a lightning flash without an end. His word is in them as they run and return. At His command, they rush like a whirlwind and bow before His Throne.

There are several wonderful images of the *Sephirot* built into this Verse: a lightning flash; running and returning; bowing; a whirlwind. From this we learn that the *Sephirot* are not static and unmoving. We tend to think of them as being immobile because, when the Tree of Life is diagrammed, each *Sephirah* is located in a certain place, along a particular path, upon its appropriate Pillar. But the Tree of Life is far from static. Like atoms and molecules and the universe itself, the *Sephirot* are so filled with energy that they do not remain still for an instant.

The Tree is often pictured as a lightning flash, as shown in Figure 3, **The Lightning Flash**. This lightning flash originates in heaven (*Keter*) and seeks ground (*Malkuth*) to discharge its energy. Lightning is a potent, terrifying force that has been associated with God(s) since ancient times. It is also a symbol of spiritual awakening, coming as it does without warning, carrying a powerful and often destructive energy, and striking where it will. The direction of this movement is vertical, going from above to below.

The second image is that of the *Sephirot* running and returning. The language used recalls Ezekiel 1:14. "And the *Chayot* running and returning, like the appearance of lightning." Ezekiel was one of Judaism's early mystics; his vision of God in His Chariot influenced Jewish mysticism for centuries. The *Chayot* are the four-faced creatures Ezekiel saw in his vision. The direction of this movement is horizontal, or side to side.

The third image is that of a whirlwind. The Hebrew word used here is *surah*, which is a hurricane that sweeps everything before it. The direction of the whirlwind's movement is circular.

The three images thus describe three different axes of movement: vertical, horizontal, and circular. Note also that the descriptions of each of these images contain a phrase that adds to the imagery of the *Sephirot*. When symbolized by a lightning flash, the *Sephirot* appear to have no end; when symbolized as running and returning, they contain God's Word; when symbolized by a whirlwind, they bow before His throne.

Taken together, we understand that the world created by the *Sephirot* appears infinite, contains God's creative power, and carries out His commands.

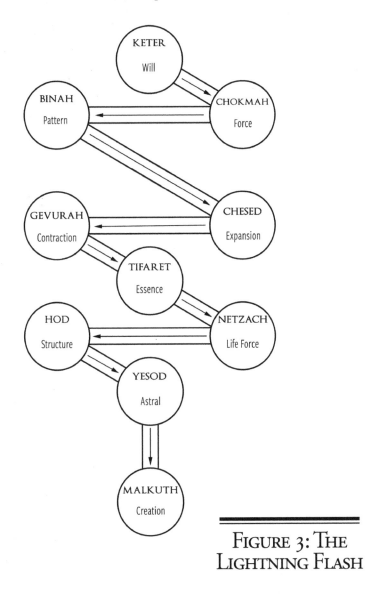

FIGURE 3: THE
LIGHTNING FLASH

Suggestions for working with Verse 1:6 ═══════════

1. Contemplate the running and returning of all created beings. As you sit, realize that thousands of beings have just departed, and thousands more have entered this life. This is an ongoing process, a constant reminder of the existence of God. Consider your own place in this progression into and out of life.

2. Consider the characteristics that Verse 1:6 ascribes to the Universe: infinite, always in motion, filled with energy, containing God's creative power and carrying out His commands. Contemplate these one at a time until you feel you understand how the Universe reflects these attributes. Now realize that in some way, each of them applies to you as well: your awareness stretches from animal awareness to divine awareness; your existence is part of God's creative power, and everything you do is at the directive of the Divine Will.

Verse 1:7 Flame Bound to a Coal

Ten Sephirot of Nothing. Their end is in their beginning and their beginning in their end, like a flame bound to a coal. The singular Master has no second; before one, what do you count?

"Their end is in their beginning and their beginning in their end" ... this is a curious phrase. It has prompted Kabbalists to wonder if the *Sefer Yetzirah* views creation as a Tree of Life followed by Tree of Life, followed by another Tree of Life, endlessly. Some envision the *Malkuth* of one Tree as the *Keter* of the Tree below it; see Figure 4, **Tree After Tree**. These Trees represent different "worlds" or planes of existence that overlap and interact with one another. In human terms, these different worlds may be understood as the body, mind, emotions and soul. All these aspects of our being overlap and interact.

Similarly, God overlaps and interacts with humanity. This interaction is symbolized by "a flame bound to a coal", an idea that is explicated further in the *Zohar*, Verses 1:50–51. "*Come and see: For YHVH your God is a devouring fire. The word has been discussed among the Companions: There is a fire devouring fire, devouring and consuming it, for there is fire fiercer than fire, as they have established. But come and see: Whoever desires to penetrate the wisdom of holy unification should contemplate the flame ascending from a glowing ember or a burning candle. For flame ascends only when grasped by a coarse substance.*"[23]

This, then, is the relationship between flame, symbolizing the spiritual world, and coal, symbolizing the physical world: coal is required to anchor and feed the flame. As flame cannot exist without coal (or fuel of some sort), so the spiritual world cannot exist without the sustenance of the physical world. It is important to realize, however, that the spiritual world and God are not one and the same. The spiritual world emanated from God, but God is far greater than the sum of both spiritual and physical worlds.

Note the apparent contradictions that arise in the text. In Verse 1:5, we

---

23 Matt, Daniel. *The Zohar, Volume 1.* Stanford, CA: Stanford University Press, 2004, pp. 282-283.

are given to understand that God is distant from humanity; in Verse 1:7, we read that God is bound to humanity. In the world of the mystic, apparent contradictions are resolved by understanding that different levels of reality are bound by different truths.

The phrase "The singular Master has no second; before One, what do you count?" reinforces the idea that there is only one God. Interestingly enough, the Tree of Life has been used to support the concept of multiple gods; it has, in fact, been used for centuries by non-Jews to support various multi-theistic belief systems. In Christian Kabbalah, for example, the first three *Sephirot* are generally assigned to the Father, Son and Holy Ghost. However, the author of the *Sefer Yetzirah* takes great pains to make it clear that, despite the multiplicity of the *Sephirot*, there is only one God.

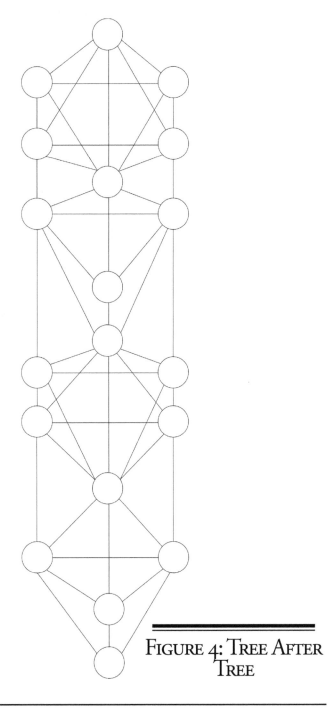

FIGURE 4: TREE AFTER TREE

Suggestions for working with Verse 1:7

1. Few of us have coal in our homes, but a candle may serve as a substitute. Light a candle; watch the flame as it dances brightly, filled with energy and light. The candle is your existence in the physical world; the flame is your soul or spiritual being. Spend some time thinking about the relationship of the candle and the flame. Can the flame exist without the candle? Does the candle serve any purpose if there is no flame?

2. The *Sefer Yetzirah* teaches that God is the number before One. The phrase "Before One, what do you count?" is a Kabbalistic koan. In Zen Buddhism, koans are small presentations of the nature of ultimate reality, usually presented as a paradox. Koans teach us that not all questions can be solved by the rational mind. Just as our minds cannot answer what number comes before the number one, so our minds cannot access God. He exists in that place where our minds cannot go.

Verse 1:8 Stop Your Mouth from Speaking

Ten Sephirot from Nothing; stop your mouth from speaking and your heart from thinking. If your heart runs, return to the place, as it is written, "running and returning." From this a covenant is made.

When we stop our mouth from speaking, our bodies are silent. When we stop our heart from thinking, we are mentally silent. As discussed in Verse 1:2, the word for "Nothing" is *blimah*, which also means "not talking." The *Sephirot* were born from silence, and it is therefore from a place of physical and mental silence that we may best approach them.

In ancient times, the heart was believed to be the seat of the mind. In fact, the idea that our thoughts originate from our hearts is mentioned in the Bible, Genesis 6:5: "The LORD saw that the wickedness of man was great in the earth, and that every intention of the thoughts of his heart was only evil continually." But no matter where our thoughts come from, it is difficult indeed to stop them. Verse 1:8 acknowledges this difficulty and suggests that when we run, i.e., when thinking begins, we should simply return to our state of no-thought, all the while recognizing that this pattern of running and returning is not just human nature but is, as we saw in Verse 1:6, part of the motion of the *Sephirot* as well. The phrase "as it is written" reminds us that this running and returning was noted originally by Ezekiel in his vision of God.

The distinguishing features of an esoteric (versus exoteric) spiritual system is the recognition that our deepest and most transformational spiritual experiences are experienced by an individual for him or herself. A second-hand report is of limited use; true spiritual experiences cannot be understood by the mind or described by language. As religious historian Karen Armstrong explains, "Some religious insights had an inner resonance that could only be apprehended by each individual in his own time during what Plato had called *theoria*, contemplation. Since all religion was directed toward an ineffable reality that lay beyond normal concepts and categories, speech was limiting and confusing. If they did not 'see' these truths with the eye of spirit, people who were not yet very experienced could get quite the wrong idea. Besides their literal meaning, therefore, the scriptures also had a spiritual significance which it was not always possible to articulate. The Buddha had also noted that certain questions were 'improper' or inappropriate, since they referred to realities that lay beyond the reach of words. You would only discover them by undergoing the introspective techniques of contemplation: in some sense, you had to create them for yourself. The attempt to describe them in words was likely to be as grotesque as a verbal account of one of Beethoven's late quartets . . . these elusive religious realities could only be suggested in the symbolic gestures of the liturgy or, better still, by silence."[24] She further notes, "There is a linguistic connection between the words 'myth,' 'mysticism,' and mystery. All are derived from the Greek verb *musteion*, to close the eyes or the mouth. All three words, therefore, are rooted in an experience of darkness and silence."[25] This silence of language and of mind is what is suggested by this Verse.

As was noted on the commentary on Verse 1.3, a covenant is a bridge between Divine and human. In this case, the bridge is created by our continuous efforts to return to the place of silence. We walk out onto this bridge of physical and mental silence to reach the *Sephirot*. The bridge is not a safe place, but we must understand that the dangers the mystic faces on this bridge lie within. There is a Kabbalistic story about four mystics who walked onto this bridge. According to the story, one died and it is generally understood that he died of fear. Another went insane as a result of his own psychic instability. The third was unable to reconcile his mystic experience with his understanding of Judaism and lost his faith. Only the fourth, Rabbi Akiva, entered into the mystic experience and emerged whole.

This parable reminds us that no matter how intelligent or accomplished we may be, mysticism is still dangerous. Whatever we bring with us into the mystic experience has the potential to cause our downfall. But Verse 1:8

---

24 Armstrong, Karen. *A History of God.* New York: Ballantine Books, 1993, pp. 114-115.

25 Armstrong, Karen. *A History of God.* New York: Ballantine Books, 1993, p. 211.

tells us that we have the opportunity to recognize and correct our weaknesses before they damage us, and this opportunity exists in silence. The point of silence is not to relax or feel good, but to have our attention forced inward, so that we are made to look at things that are normally hidden or glossed over. Silence has the potential to gift us with a deep understanding of our own inner selves and to bring healing to old injuries.

Suggestions for working with Verse 1:8

1. Create an opportunity to experience an entire day of physical silence, understanding that such opportunities are not part of everyday life and must be created deliberately, sometimes with great effort. It is rarely possible to do this in the normal context of home and work. Ideally, go to a silent retreat and experience several days of community silence. If this is not an option, spend a day alone in nature, at a park, or at home if you can be alone. Take the opportunity to spend time with yourself, watching what arises for you. Resist the urge to chronicle your thoughts in a journal until the day is over; writing relieves the internal pressure that is necessary to this process.

2. One of *Keter's* many images is that of a bearded king seen in profile. We see part of the king's face, but the other part will always be hidden from us. How is this image an accurate reflection of God? How is this image an accurate reflection of ourselves?

Verse 1:9 Ruach of the Living God

Ten Sephirot from Nothing. One—the Ruach of the Living God, blessed and praised is the name of He who gives life to the worlds. Voice, spirit and word are the Holy Ruach.

This is the first in a series of ten descriptions which are generally believed to refer to the *Sephirot*; this Verse is generally, though not universally, thought to refer to *Keter*, the first *Sephirah* on the Tree.

The Hebrew word *Ruach* can mean wind, air, breath or spirit, terms which are conceptually intertwined. Wind is, of course, moving air, and air is what we breathe. Our breath has always been connected with spirit because when our spirit leaves our body, our breathing stops. Breath is also associated with life and creation: the word "inspiration" literally means to "breathe in", and it is this giving of life that is associated with the energy of God.

In the last sentence, our unknown author further relates *Ruach* to voice, spirit and word. Just as "spirit" is related to breath and air, voice and word are similarly related. Since the *Sefer Yetzirah* understands language to be the instrument of creation, it identifies voice and word with God's *Ruach* or creative energy. Thus, Holy *Ruach* (*Ruach Elohim* in Hebrew) is generally translated as "Breath of God" or "Spirit of God." The *Ruach Elohim* is what moved on the face of the water in Genesis 1:2, before God said *Lehi Or*, "Let there be light." *Ruach Elohim* also provides understanding, knowledge, skill and ability. The term is used in Exodus 31:3, in which God says He has filled Betzalel, the builder of the tabernacle, with the *Ruach Elohim*, giving Betzalel the knowledge and skills required to build the tabernacle.

In the second sentence, the phrase "blessed and praised" uses the Hebrew words *baruch* and *m'vorakh*. Both these words come from the root word meaning "blessed," though *m'vorakh* may be more accurately translated as "from blessing." As noted by Aryeh Kaplan, *baruch* means blessed by nature, while *m'vorakh* means blessed by others. Thus, we understand that God is blessed both by His own nature and by humankind.

The idea of humankind blessing God is often difficult for us to appreciate. How can it be appropriate for mere humans to bless God? What does it even mean? The key here is that the word "bless" means two different things depending on which way the blessing is traveling. A blessing may mean a special gift or favor: when God blesses us, this is usually what we are hoping for. However, a blessing may also mean approval and affirmation: when we bless God, we are affirming His power, mercy or some other quality that we approve of. Perhaps the blessings we receive are contingent upon the blessings we give.

Suggestions for working with Verse 1:9

1. The use of the word *ruach* for spirit, air, breath, voice and word provides wonderful opportunity for contemplation. For example, air is necessary to life. Our thoughts seem to travel on air, as does sound and language. Both our thoughts and our words have creative power, defining us and allowing us to express ourselves to the world. Contemplate the relationship between spirit, air, breath, voice and word. How do the concepts of air, breath, voice and word deepen our understanding of spirit?

2. God asks for our blessing not because He needs it, but because we benefit from the act of blessing God. Contemplate how blessing God (or our fellow humans) benefits us.

Verse 1:10 Ruach from Ruach

Two: ruach from Ruach. He engraved and hewed in it twenty-two foundation letters—three mothers, seven double, and twelve simple— and Ruach is the first of them.

Remember that *Ruach* can be translated a number of different ways— wind, air, breath or spirit—and in this case, the preferred translation is "air". *Ruach* can also be used to describe God, in the context of the Breath, Spirit, Voice and Word of God. The phrase "*ruach* from *Ruach*" teaches that air (*ruach*) comes from God (*Ruach*).

The phrase at the end, "...and *Ruach* is the first of them" refers to the first of the Hebrew letters, *Aleph*, which is believed to be responsible for the creation of air. In other words, the Breath or Voice of God (*Ruach*) created the element of air through the medium of the Hebrew letter *Aleph*. In Verse 1:1, we read that creation occurs through numbers, letters and their expression; this is the first example of this means of creation. The letter *Aleph* is expressed by the Voice or Breath of God (*Ruach*), resulting in the element of air.

Verses 1:11 and 1:12 will introduce the other two Kabbalistic elements: water and fire. Most of us are familiar with the Aristotelian system of four elements (fire, air, water, earth) and the Chinese system of five elements (metal, water, wood, fire and earth); the *Sefer Yetzirah* system is based on three elements.

One of the key concepts of the *Sefer Yetzirah* is that things come into being via stages, or levels, of reality. A frog emanates from a tadpole which emanates from an egg; similarly, all things that exist in the physical world have emanated from something that once existed on a different level. And, despite differences in structure, form and appearance, they are essentially the same thing: the frog, the tadpole and the egg are one: the same species, breed, and identity. This concept lies at the very heart of the *Sefer Yetzirah*. The first sentence, "*ruach* from *Ruach*", affirms that *Ruach* emanates from one level to another level, transforming God's Voice into air.

The words "engraved and hewed" or "engraved and carved" describe how God formed the universe, and refer to two different "scales" of creation: fine and coarse. God creates on an unimaginably small scale (atoms) as well as on an immeasurably large scale (galaxies).

Suggestions for working with Verse 1:10

1. *Ruach* is the Breath, Spirit, Voice and Word of God as well as the air, life, breath, and spirit of humanity. Contemplate how these different aspects of *Ruach* are all around and within us.

2. Just as God both "hewed" (created on a large scale) and "engraved" (created on a small scale), we too create large experiences and small ones. Consider the large and small aspects of your own life; remember that experiences that appear to be small and irrelevant may, in their emanations, be surprisingly significant.

Verse 1:11 Water from Ruach

Three: water from Ruach. He engraved and hewed them from Tohu and Bohu, mud and clay. He made them like a bed, like a wall, like a roof. He put coldness upon them and made earth, as it reads, "He said to the snow, 'Become earth.'"

In the previous Verse, we read that the element of air was created (through the medium of *Aleph*) from the Holy *Ruach*.

The next element created by God was water, which emanated from air. Earth emanated from water, specifically frozen water. The fact that earth is part of water and not considered an element in and of itself is shown in the phrase, "He put coldness upon them and made earth, as it reads, 'He said to the snow, 'Become earth.'"

This concept is also seen in Genesis 1:9. "God said, 'Let the water below the sky be gathered into one area, that the dry land may appear.'" God creates light, water and sky, but He does not create land; this is because land emanates from water.

The phrase "*Tohu* and *Bohu*" comes from Genesis 1:2 and is usually translated as "chaos." Another ancient Kabbalistic text called the *Sefer Bahir* differentiates between these two words: "What is Chaos (*Tohu*)? Something that confounds (*Taha*) people. What is desolation (*Bohu*)? It is something that has substance."[26] *Bohu*, which has substance, came from *Tohu*, which is chaos; similarly, earth, which is substantial, came from water, which is chaotic.

The *Sefer Bahir* adds, "He created Desolation (*Bohu*) and placed it in Peace, and He created Chaos (*Tohu*) and placed it in Evil."[27] *Tohu* is placed in Evil; from a Kabbalistic viewpoint, this means that it forms the Female Pillar, while *Bohu* is placed in Peace, i.e., forms the Male Pillar. Though Genesis would have us believe that the world was originally chaos and God created order, the *Sefer Bahir* notes that chaos also must have been created by God.

26 Kaplan, Aryeh. *The Bahir: Illumination.* York Beach, ME: Samuel Weiser, Inc., 1979, p. 1.

27 Kaplan, Aryeh. *The Bahir: Illumination.* York Beach, ME: Samuel Weiser, Inc., 1979, p. 5.

Some scholars think the garden bed, wall and roof are various aspects of Hebrew calligraphy. However, it may be more useful for the spiritual aspirant to view the garden bed, wall and roof as the dimensions of space: breadth, depth and width. The bed, wall and roof may also be considered as representations of the Tree of Life: *Malkuth* acts as the fertile garden bed, *Keter* as the roof of the sky above and the other *Sephirot* as walls.

Suggestions for working with Verse 1:11

1. Contemplate the following from the Prophet Isaiah (55:9–11).
"But as the heavens are high above the earth,
So are My ways high above your ways
And My plans above your plans.
For as the rain or snow drops from heaven
And returns not there,
But soaks the earth
And makes it bring forth vegetation,
Yielding seed for sowing and bread for eating,
So is the word that issues from My mouth:
It does not come back to Me unfulfilled,
But performs what I purpose,
Achieves what I sent it to do."

Everything that occurs in the world does so because God's Words obey His Purpose or Will. This Verse cautions us that God's ways are not our ways, despite the belief that man is a microcosm of the great Macrocosm. There is great wisdom hidden here for the seeker.

Verse 1:12 Fire from Ruach

Four: fire from water. As He formed for Himself the Throne of Glory, Serafim, Ofanim and the Holy Animals as the Ministering Angels, so from the three He made His dwelling, as it is written, "He makes winds his angels, and flames of fire his servants." [Psalms 104:4]

The element of fire emanates from the element of water. This emanation is a conceptual rather than literal device.

The phrase "Throne of Glory" refers to Ezekiel's vision of God riding on a mighty Throne or Chariot (Ezekiel 1:26). This vision constitutes an essential part of *merkavah* (meaning chariot) mysticism, upon which modern Kabbalah is founded. *Ofanim* refer to the wheels of the Chariot and the Holy Animals are the four *Cherubim*, a classification of angel, who held the Chariot up. Each *Cherub* had four faces—man, ox, eagle and lion—which is why they're known as the Holy Animals. These four faces provide another reference to the number four.

The *Serafim*, another classification of angel, are associated with the Throne of Glory as described in Isaiah 6:1–3: "... I saw the Lord sitting upon a throne, high and lifted up; and His train filled the Hekhal [sanctuary]. Above Him stood the Seraphim; each had six wings: with two he covered his face, and with two he covered his feet, and with two he flew." The word *Serafim* comes from the Hebrew root *saraf*, which means "to burn": their inclusion adds additional emphasis to this Verse's theme of fire.

The phrase "so from the three He made His dwelling" refers to the three elements of air, water and fire, as is confirmed by the quote from Psalms 104:4, "He makes winds his angels, and flames of fire his servants." Verse 1:12 is drawing a parallel between the two places where God sits: His Throne (formed with *Serafim*, *Ofanim*, and Holy Animals) and the Earth (referred to in this Verse as God's dwelling and formed with air, water and fire).

Life can exist only after all the elements are in place. Verse 1:10 brought us the element of air; Verse 1:11 brought the element of water; Verse 1:12 brings us fire. The rest of creation can now come into being.

Suggestions for working with Verse 1:12

1. Speak the Verse aloud; then sit quietly, keeping the words in your mind. There is no need to memorize it; look at the text whenever you feel uncertain of the words.

2. In drawing a parallel between the God's Throne (formed with angelic beings like *Serafim*, *Ofanim*, and Holy Animals) and the Earth (formed with air, water, and fire), Verse 1:12 invites us to see the air, water and fire around us as divine. Spend some time each day learning to see these elements differently.

Verse 1:13 Sealing the Six Extremities

He chose three of the simple letters, the secret of the three Mothers: Aleph Mem Shin. He put them in His Great Name and with them sealed the six extremities. Five: He sealed above, facing upward, and sealed it with Yod Heh Vav. Six: He sealed below, facing downward, and sealed it with Heh Yod Vav. Seven: He sealed east, facing straight ahead and sealed it with Vav Yod Heh. Eight: He sealed west, facing backward and sealed it with Vav Heh Yod. Nine: He sealed south, facing to the right and sealed it with Yod Vav Heh. Ten: He sealed north, facing to the left and sealed it with Heh Vav Yod.

This Verse states that the three simple or mother letters, *Aleph*, *Mem* and *Shin*, were chosen to be put into the Great Name; but we also know that the Great Name consists of the three letters *Yod*, *Heh* and *Vav*, all of which are simple or single letters. This apparent contradiction is resolved by understanding that, when the mother letters were placed into the Great Name, they were transformed into *Yod*, *Heh* and *Vav*.

To make sense of this transmutation, we must realize that, according to the *Sefer Yetzirah*, the three elements were created by the three mother letters. This teaching isn't stated outright until Verse 3:2, but the ancient author presumes that his readers already know this. *Aleph* created air, *Mem* created water, and *Shin* created fire. It is believed that these three letters were selected because the word *avir*, meaning air, starts with an *Aleph*; *mayim*, meaning water, starts with a *Mem*; *aish*, meaning fire, contains a *Shin*.

Aleph and air are neutral and genderless, *Mem* and water are positive and male, and *Shin* and fire are negative and female. In terms of modern Kabbalah and the Tree of Life, *Aleph* is assigned to the Middle Pillar, *Mem* is the Male Pillar, and *Shin* is the Female Pillar. (As we shall learn in Chapter 3, the three mother letters are also assigned to the three horizontal paths of the Tree.)

While the exact match between the *Aleph Mem Shin* triad and the *Yod*

Heh Vav triad is not provided in this Verse, it was, again, generally understood that *Mem* (water and male) was transformed into *Yod*, a letter often associated with the phallus. *Aleph* (air and neutral) was transformed into *Vav*. The rationale for this transformation is that both *Aleph* and *Vav* are connecting letters: *Aleph* represents the Middle Pillar which connects the Male and Female Pillars, while *Vav* means "and" in Hebrew and thus connects words. By default, then, *Shin* (fire and female) was transformed into *Heh*.

The Verse draws a parallel between the creation of the physical world with the three mother letters and the sealing or closing of that world's six boundaries with the three letters of the Great Name. The term used here for seals is *chotmot*; Glotzer explains that the word means both "completion" and "knot."[28] The six directions are thus knotted together, completing the three dimensions of physical space. The world is limited per God's direction and bound with God's name; legend has it that God stood at the site of the Temple in Jerusalem when He sealed the six directions.

Suggestions for working with Verse 1:13

1. Notice that the phrasing of this Verse gives the impression that God sealed Himself into these six boundaries, as He was evidently standing at the center when He created the seals. What aspect of God might we think of as sealed inside the six boundaries? What aspect is outside the six boundaries?

2. Stand in the center of a room and imagine that you stand at the very center of the universe, facing east. Look up to the ceiling and picture this direction as infinite and without end. Then chant "*Yod Heh Vav*" aloud and imagine that you have just created a wall that limits this direction. Look down at the floor and picture this direction as infinite and without end.

---

28 Glotzer, Leonard R. *The Fundamentals of Jewish Mysticism: The Book of Creation and Its Commentaries.*
Northvale, NJ: Jason Aronson, Inc., 1992, p. 60.

Then chant "*Heh Yod Vav*"aloud and imagine that you have just created a wall that limits this direction.

Face straight ahead (east) and picture this direction as infinite and without end. Then chant "*Vav Yod Heh*"aloud and imagine that you have just created a wall that limits this direction. Turn to face the west and picture this direction as infinite and without end. Then chant "*Vav Heh Yod*"aloud and imagine that you have just created a wall that limits this direction.

Turn to face the south and picture this direction as infinite and without end. Then chant "*Yod Vav Heh*"aloud and imagine that you have just created a wall that limits this direction. Turn to face the north and picture this direction as infinite and without end. Then chant "*Heh Vav Yod*"aloud and imagine that you have just created a wall that limits this direction.

Conclude this practice by standing at the center of this newly created universe and consider what walls and limits exist in your own life. What aspect of your self is sealed within? What aspect lies without?

Verse 1:14 Summary of Chapter One

These are the ten Sephirot of Nothing: the Ruach of the living God; air; water; fire; height; depth; east; west; north; south.

This Verse is a summary of Chapter One. It divides the ten *Sephirot* into *Ruach*, three elements, and six directions.

Linking the concepts of the *Sefer Yetzirah* to the Tree of Life is often helpful to modern students. Since the *Sefer Yetzirah* does not tell us which of the *Sephirot* correspond to which of the three elements or six boundaries of space, and since our modern version of the Tree was probably unknown at the time the *Sefer Yetzirah* was written, we are free to create correspondences that suit our understanding. One set of correspondences that works fairly well is this:

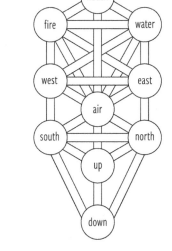

Keter: *Ruach*

Chokmah: water

Binah: fire

Chesed: east

Gevurah: west

Tifaret: air

Netzach: north

Hod: south

Yesod: up

Malkuth: down

In this list, water is placed in the Male Pillar, fire in the Female Pillar and air, the mediating element, is placed at the very heart of the Tree on the Middle Pillar. Also, since air emanated from *Ruach*, air's position in *Tifaret*, directly below *Ruach* in *Keter*, is appropriate. "Down" is assigned to *Malkuth*, making *Yesod* an obvious selection for "up".

Suggestions for working with Verse 1:14

1. Stand and contemplate your own *ruach*: your life, desire and will. Feel the connection of your own *ruach* to the *Ruach Elohim* that brought the entire world into being. Then expand your awareness to the *ruach* of the entire planet.

Then move your awareness to the contemplation of the air moving into and out of your lungs. Expand that contemplation to include the air moving in and out of the many billions of lungs of all the creatures on this planet.

Next, move your awareness to the contemplation of water in your body and the blood circulating through your veins. Expand that contemplation to include all the water on the planet—seas, lakes, rivers, clouds and all physical beings.

Next, move your awareness to the contemplation of fire in your body: your inner body temperature and the warmth you feel on your skin as your body exudes heat. Then move your attention outward to the fire that exists throughout the planet, from a forest fire that is undoubtedly raging somewhere at this moment to the boiling contents of the earth's inner core.

To contemplate height, move your awareness above the top of your head, to the auric crown you wear. Then move your attention outward and consider the farthest reaches of the planet's atmosphere.

Add the dimension of depth by experiencing the way in which your body is rooted to the ground through your feet. Then move your attention downward to experience the depth of the planet itself.

Experience the dimension of east by sending your awareness to your right hand, feeling the power and dexterity of this hand. Add west by shifting your awareness to your left hand, feeling the power and dexterity of that hand. Then move your attention outward to experience the easternmost and westernmost parts of the world.

Contemplate north by becoming aware of the front of your body and its accompanying feeling of openness and attention. Contemplate south by becoming aware of the back of your body, its strength and support. Then move your attention outward to experience the northernmost and southernmost parts of the world.

Through exercises such as this one we learn to dissolve the barriers of our perceived individuality and become part of a larger whole.

Chapter Two
The Twenty-Two Letters

Chapter Two gives us more information about the twenty-two letters and teaches us an important contemplative technique called the 231 Gates.

Verse 2:1 Three Mother Letters

Twenty-two foundation letters: three mothers, seven doubles, and twelve simple letters. Three mothers, Aleph Mem Shin: their foundation is the scale of merit and deficit, the pointer balances the two. Three mothers, Aleph Mem Shin: Mem is silent, Shin is sibilant, Aleph is the air that balances the two.

Verse 2:1 reminds us that there are twenty-two foundation letters—three mother letters, seven double letters and twelve simple (or single) letters—and explains that the three mother letters are *Aleph*, *Mem* and *Shin*. The letters *Mem* and *Shin* are assigned, respectively, to merit and deficit, which we may also think of as positive and negative, thesis and antithesis, water and fire, etc. *Aleph* represents balance, neutrality or a point of resolution between opposing forces. *Aleph*, *Mem* and *Shin* thus represent the triad of positive/negative/neutral or thesis/antithesis/resolution. (A similar system is found in the Vedic *Gunas*: *Rajas* is the quality of activity; *Tamas* is the quality of inertia; *Sattva* is the quality of balance. The *Gunas* are regarded as the three major operating principles of nature.)

Note the sounds made by the letters: *Mem* sounds like an "m", a soothing, humming sound; *Shin* sounds like "sh", a hissing, irritating sound; *Aleph* is a silent letter with no sound at all. These sounds seem to reflect the associated qualities of merit, deficit and balance.

The Hebrew word used here for "scale" is *kaf*, which may also mean the palm of the hand. The Hebrew word that has been translated here as "pointer" is *lashon*; this may also be translated as "tongue." The metaphor in this case urges each of us to see ourselves as a scale, with our two hands as pans and our tongue as the pointer in the middle. The idea of the tongue as the pointer teaches us that our language reflects our actions, as the tongue is the pointer between the pans, or, carrying the idea further, that language can alter our actions, a concept very much in keeping with the magical aspects of the text. Recall that in Verse 1:3 we learned that the "word of the tongue" is part of the "covenant in the center" and that the tongue is an organ of creation.

Suggestions for working with Verse 2:1

1. Use the letter *Mem* as a chant to bring yourself closer to the Pillar of Mercy. *Mem* may be regarded as a Hebrew version of the Hindu meditation word "om". Similarly, you can use the letter *Shin* to bring yourself close to the Pillar of Severity. Students often ask why we would want to move closer to the Pillar of Severity; remember that the ideal of the Kabbalist is not virtue, mercy or mildness, but *balance*. We are taught that Abraham was told to sacrifice Isaac because Abraham was out of balance: too close to the Pillar of Mercy (specifically the *Sephirah* of *Chesed*) and too far from the Pillar of Severity (specifically the *Sephirah* of *Gevurah*). The near-sacrifice of Isaac injected some much-needed *Gevurah* into Abraham's character. Being out of balance on the side of mercy is believed by Kabbalists to be as grave a fault as being out of balance on the side of restriction.

Note that to perform this exercise, we must first determine whether we are closer to the Pillar of Mercy or to the Pillar of Severity. This requires an honest assessment of our character and the way in which we relate to ourselves and those around us. If you are not certain whether you should chant *Mem* or *Shin*, another alternative is to chant the letter *Aleph*. Since the letter *Aleph* is a silent letter, the practice of chanting *Aleph* is a Kabbalistic *koan*: what does a silent letter chant sound like?

Verse 2:2 Six Verbs of Creation

Twenty-two letters: He engraved them, hewed them, weighed them, interchanged them, combined them, and formed with them all that was created and all that would be created.

These six verbs—engraved, hewed, weighed, interchanged, combined and formed—are used throughout the *Sefer Yetzirah* to describe the means by which the foundational letters created the world. The use of these six verbs reinforces the concept of creation as a complex process. Creation requires a wide variety of activities: desire, will, knowledge, understanding, contemplation, effort, physical action, time, etc. All these processes are involved in creating a sculpture, a painting, a symphony, a book, a meal, a building, and so on.

Engraving, the first step in creation, is will or desire. The act of creation rests on both the desire to create and the will to see it through. The second step, hewing, is knowledge: we must have knowledge of the letters, which we obtain through study and writing. The third step, weighing, requires us to grasp the intrinsic nature of each letter and its creative potential before we can actually use that letter to create. This is done by prolonged contemplation. The fourth stage, interchanging, is the process by which we learn to view the letter as equivalent to that which it will create. At this level, when we see the letter *Aleph*, for example, we immediately see that which it creates: air, neutrality, resolution. At this stage, the letters begin their creative processes, though only in our minds. Combining brings the desired creation into a fully formed concept; forming brings the letter into space-time-human reality and the process is complete.

The idea of six stages of creation may seem cumbersome, and indeed, most of us leap into things without much thought. We can see, however, that utilizing these six stages would help us create more thoughtfully and more successfully in our own lives. For example, if we decide to get a new job, we can just hunt through the want ads and apply for whichever one pays the best; but a better job might be obtained by carefully going through the six stages described in this Verse. The first stage would be the deisre for a new job and the will to begin searching. The second stage would be becoming knowledgeable about our options. The third stage would be developing a deep understanding about what we need this new job to bring into our lives. The fourth stage would be comparing potential employers and job offers. The fifth stage would be the selection of the new job. The sixth stage would be starting work at that new job.

When applied to the study of the Hebrew letters, this Verse inspires a variety of contemplative and magical practices. "Engraving" is done by chanting, as is made clear in the next Verse. "Hewing" refers to physically writing the letters. "Weighing" requires us to focus on the letters in our mind's eye, using visualization techniques. "Interchanging" refers to the consciously created link between the letter and its space-time equivalent. "Combining" the letters is a more complex visualization technique in which the letters interact with one another and blend together in our minds, resulting in more complex creative possibilities. "Forming" is a resulting change in space, time or humanity. As a result of these six practices, the letters become something more substantial. Just as God engraved, hewed, weighed, interchanged, combined and formed *Aleph* into air and the mediating influence between merit and deficit, so we too may engrave, hew, weigh, interchange, combine and form the letters to create for ourselves.

It has been suggested that these different ways of working with the letters may have an influence on different dimensions of reality. Writing, chanting and visualizing the letters may influence the three-dimensional physical realm. The practice of "interchanging" may affect the dimension of time. The practice of "combining" may change the dimension of humanity.

In order to work with the Hebrew letters, it is necessary for the student to be able to recognize and, eventually, to write the letters. If you are not yet familiar with the Hebrew letters, see Table 1, **Hebrew Letters**, for a list of the letters and their associate numbers.

Table 1: Hebrew Letters

Symbol	Name	Number
א	Aleph	1
ב	Bet	2
ג	Gimel	3
ד	Dalet	4
ה	Heh	5
ו	Vav	6
ז	Zayin	7
ח	Chet	8
ט	Tet	9
י	Yod	10
כ	Kaph	20
ל	Lamed	30
מ	Mem	40
נ	Nun	50
ס	Samech	60
ע	Ayin	70
פ	Peh	80
צ	Tzadi	90
ק	Kuf	100
ר	Resh	200
ש	Shin	300
ת	Tav	400

Suggestions for working with this Verse:

1. Contemplate the Verse for 15 minutes. Start by speaking the Verse aloud; then sit quietly, keeping the words in your mind. There is no need to memorize it; look at the text whenever you feel uncertain of the words.

2. Chant the Hebrew letters *Aleph* and *Bet* several times, sinking into the sound of the letters. Write the letters over and over, until you feel that you know them well. Then close your eyes and bring up *Aleph* in your mind's eye. Having done that, release it and bring up *Bet*. Then bring both letters into your mind. Once you have them firmly established, bring them close together until they touch and then intertwine. Allow them to take on a life of their own. They may vanish or they may form something entirely different. Pay attention to the ideas, thoughts, pictures or realizations that come to you.

Verse 2:3 Five Places in the Mouth

Twenty-two letters of foundation are engraved in sound, hewn in wind, fixed in five places in the mouth: (1) Aleph, Chet, Hey, Ayin in the throat; (2) Gimel, Yod, Kaf, Kuf at the palate; (3) Dalet, Tet, Lamed, Nun, Tav on the tongue; (4) Zayin, Samech, Shin, Resh, Tzadi on the teeth; (5) Bet, Vav, Mem, Peh on the lips.

The *Sefer Yetzirah* typically divides the twenty-two letters into the three groups of mothers, doubles and elementals, but this Verse deviates from that norm by dividing the twenty-two letters into five groups based on the way in which they are formed in the mouth: the letters may be sounded from the throat, palate, tongue, teeth and lips. Note the order in which the letters are presented; the letters come from within, beginning with the throat; they move outward to the palate, then the tongue, then the teeth and finally the lips. This teaches us that language, like all creative processes, begins within and is then directed outward.

Different translations give us more insight into the nature and intent of the actions God took with respect to the 22 letters:

"He ordained them by voice, He hewed them from spirit, He fixed them in the mouth..."[29]

"...designed in the voice, formed in the air and set in the mouth..."[30]

"...formed by the voice, impressed on the air, and audibly modified..."[31]

29 Friedman, Irving. *The Book of Creation.* New York, NY: Samuel Weiser, Inc., 1977, p. 5.

30 Kalisch, Rev. Dr. Isidor and Stenring, Knut. *Sepher Yetzirah: The Book of Creation.* San Diego, CA: The Book Tree, 2006, p. 80.

31 Westcott, W. Wynn. *Sepher Yetzirah: The Book of Formation and the 32 Paths of Wisdom.* Kessinger Publishing's Rare Reprints, p. 18.

"…He engraved them with voice[,] He carved them with breath[,] He set them in the mouth…"[32]

The metaphysical point being made by the author involves the progression from non-physical to physical, from designing and forming to setting and fixing, from God to man. Verse 2:3 thereby provides us with a model of God's creative process using speech as a metaphor. It begins when He ordains or designs the letters (voicing the letters); then hews, carves or impresses them (shaping the sound of the letters with His Breath); and finally fixes the letters in His Mouth (articulating the letters with different parts of His Mouth). Another way to read this Verse is that the final act of God's speech process is the placing of the letters in the mouth of *mankind*: the final act of creation is ours.

Suggestions for working with Verse 2:3

1. Consider the processes that result in your use of spoken language. Where does the impulse to speak actually begin? Does it begin with a thought? With a feeling? With a need of some kind? Understanding what prompts us to speak—and thereby create—can help us to change the nature of the life we are creating.

---

32 Kaplan, Aryeh. *Sefer Yetzirah: The Book of Creation.* York Beach, ME: Samuel Weiser, Inc., 1997, p. 102.

Verse 2:4 231 Gates

Twenty-two Foundation Letters are fixed in a circle with 231 Gates. The Circle is turned back and forth. A sign for this is that there is nothing in good better than joy (Oneg: Ayin Nun Gimel) and there is nothing in evil worse than plague (Nega: Nun Gimel Ayin).

Verses 2:4 and 2:5 introduce the concept of the 231 Gates, a contemplative technique that has been used by Kabbalists for centuries. These 231 Gates are the two hundred and thirty-one two-letter combinations that can be created from the twenty-two Hebrew letters. The Gates are formed by taking the first letter, *Aleph*, and combining it with all the other letters in the alphabet, which results in 21 different combinations. This first set of 21 Gates, called the *Aleph* Gates, are shown in Figure 5, **Aleph Gates**. Next comes the second letter, *Bet*, which is similarly combined with all the other letters of the alphabet. But, since one of those combinations, *Aleph Bet*, is already part of the *Aleph* Gates, there are only 20 new combinations in the *Bet* Gates. (See Figure 6, **Bet Gates**.) When we take the third letter, *Gimel*, and combine it with the other letters in the alphabet, there will be two combinations which were previously produced—*Aleph Gimel* and *Bet Gimel*—creating only 19 new combinations. (See Figure 7, **Gimel Gates**.) When we add up the number of Gates derived in this manner, we get 21 + 20 + 19 + 18 + 17 + 16 + 15 + 14 + 13 + 12 + 11 + 10 + 9 + 8 + 7 + 6 + 5 + 4 + 3 + 2 + 1 = 231 combinations. These Gates are shown in Figure 8, **231 Gates**.

Verse 2:4 also teaches us that when the letters are reversed they produce an opposite meaning. The example given in this Verse is the Hebrew word for "joy", *Oneg* (*Ayin Nun Gimel*), which is contrasted with the Hebrew word for "affliction", *Negah* (*Nun Gimel Ayin*). Hebrew words are based on roots of three letters, rather than two letters, but applying the concept of reversal to our 231 Gates suggests that Gate *Aleph Bet* would create one thing, while *Bet Aleph* would create its opposite. The letters in Figures 5, 6, and 7 are arranged counter-clockwise around the circle, in recognition of the fact that Hebrew is read from right to left rather than left to right. We would reverse the letters by arranging them around the circle from right to left, as shown in Figure 9, **Reverse *Aleph* Gates**.

This ancient Kabbalistic technique can provide a profound experience for modern students. These two-letter combinations are called "Gates" because they are doorways to alternate states of being. Each set of "Gates" forms a unique doorway which is related to the creative power of the letter. Of this we will speak no further, for the intent is for the student to experience the Gates for him or herself, not to suggest what should be experienced.

FIGURE 5: ALEPH GATES

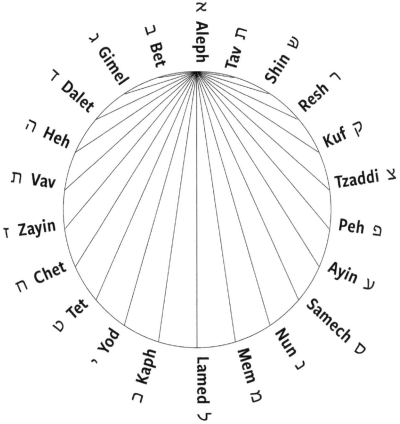

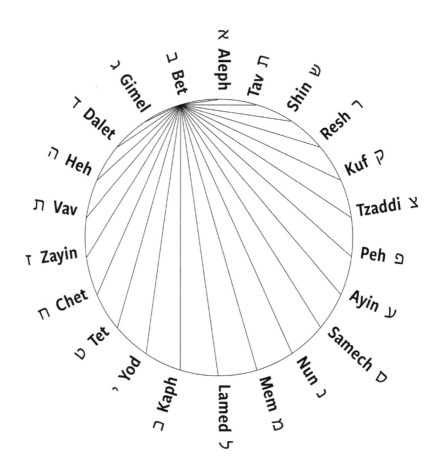

FIGURE 6: BET GATES

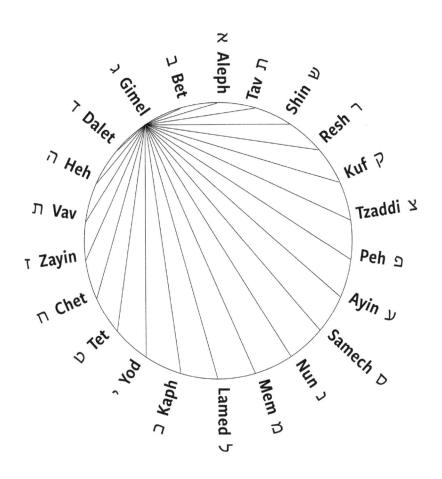

FIGURE 7: GIMEL
GATES

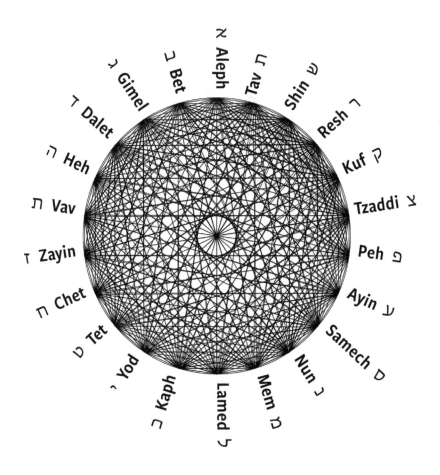

FIGURE 8: 231
GATES

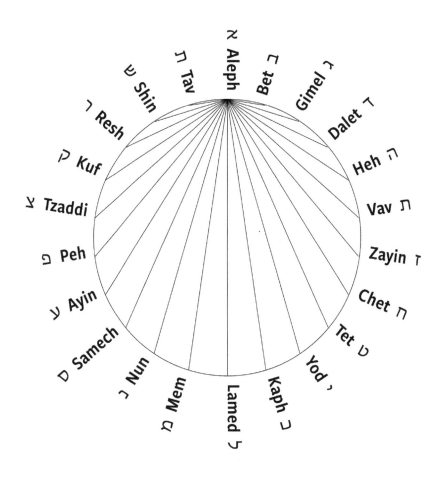

FIGURE 9: REVERSE
ALEPH GATES

Suggestions for working with Verse 2:4 ═══════

1. Using Figure 5, *Aleph* **Gates**, chant the 22 *Aleph* Gates: *Aleph Bet, Aleph Gimel, Aleph Dalet, Aleph Heh*, etc. Persevere until you have overcome your unfamiliarity with the letters: soon you will find that this chant has a deeply calming effect.

2. Using Figure 9, **Reverse** *Aleph* **Gates**, chant the 22 *Aleph* Gates in reverse order: *Aleph Tav, Aleph Shin, Aleph Resh*, etc. Note if and how this chanting exercise feels different from the previous one, or if it results in bringing you to a different place in your awareness. Do you feel less calm? More calm?

Verse 2:5 Aleph with All of Them

How did He combine, weigh, and interchange them? Aleph with all of them and all of them with Aleph, Bet with all of them and all of them with Bet, and so on. There are 231 Gates, and all creation and all language emerge from One Name.

All of creation emerges from the various combinations of the Hebrew letters; everything emerges from the 231 Gates. The letters are regarded as atoms, which combine to produce molecules which, in turn, combine to produce the stuff of life. All creation and all the languages in the world emerge from the One Name, meaning everything derives from the one alphabet and thus the One God. Again, the *Sefer Yetzirah* is attempting to stress the unity of creation.

Many Kabbalists have considered the "One Name" as a reference to the four-letter name of God known as the Tetragrammaton (*Yod Heh Vav Heh*). This has led to the creation of complex combinations of Hebrew letters using the four letters of the Tetragrammaton and the twenty-two letters of the Hebrew alphabet, or the four letters of the Tetragrammaton and Hebrew vowels, which are not among the twenty-two letters of the Hebrew alphabet.

Suggestions for working with Verse 2:5

1. Contemplate the Verse for 15 minutes. Start by speaking the Verse aloud; then sit quietly, keeping the words in your mind. There is no need to memorize it; look at the text whenever you feel uncertain of the words.

2. Using Table 2, **22 Letters and the Tetragrammaton**, chant the combinations of each Hebrew letter with the letter *Yod*: *Aleph Yod, Bet Yod, Gimel Yod, Dalet Yod, Heh Yod, Vav Yod*, etc. Then chant the combinations of each Hebrew letter with the letter *Heh*: *Aleph Heh, Bet Heh, Gimel Heh, Dalet Heh, Heh Heh, Vav Heh*, etc. Then chant the combinations of each

Hebrew letter with the letter *Vav: Aleph Vav, Bet Vav, Gimel Vav, Dalet Vav, Heh Vav, Vav Vav*, etc. Finally, repeat the chant of the combinations of each Hebrew letter with the letter *Heh: Aleph Heh, Bet Heh, Gimel Heh, Dalet Heh, Heh Heh, Vav Heh*, etc.

TABLE 2: 22 LETTERS AND THE TETRAGRAMMATON

Aleph Yod	*Aleph Heh*	*Aleph Vav*	*Aleph Heh*
Bet Yod	*Bet Heh*	*Bet Vav*	*Bet Heh*
Gimel Yod	*Gimel Heh*	*Gimel Vav*	*Gimel Heh*
Dalet Yod	*Dalet Heh*	*Dalet Vav*	*Dalet Heh*
Heh Yod	*Vav Heh*	*Heh Vav*	*Vav Heh*
Vav Yod	*Zayin Heh*	*Zayin Vav*	*Zayin Heh*
Zayin Yod	*Chet Heh*	*Chet Vav*	*Chet Heh*
Chet Yod	*Tet Heh*	*Tet Vav*	*Tet Heh*
Tet Yod	*Yod Heh*	*Yod Vav*	*Yod Heh*
Kaph Yod	*Kaph Heh*	*Kaph Vav*	*Kaph Heh*
Lamed Yod	*Lamed Heh*	*Lamed Vav*	*Lamed Heh*
Mem Yod	*Mem Heh*	*Mem Vav*	*Mem Heh*
Nun Yod	*Nun Heh*	*Nun Vav*	*Nun Yod*
Samech Yod	*Samech Heh*	*Samech Vav*	*Samech Yod*
Ayin Yod	*Ayin Heh*	*Ayin Vav*	*Ayin Yod*
Peh Yod	*Peh Heh*	*Peh Vav*	*Peh Heh*
Tzaddi Yod	*Tzaddi Heh*	*Tzaddi Vav*	*Tzaddi Heh*
Kuf Yod	*Kuf Heh*	*Kuf Vav*	*Kuf Heh*
Resh Yod	*Resh Heh*	*Resh Vav*	*Resh Heh*
Shin Yod	*Shin Heh*	*Shin Vav*	*Shin Heh*
Tav Yod	*Tav Heh*	*Tav Vav*	*Tav Heh*

Verse 2:6 Great Pillars

He formed substance from chaos and made nonexistence into existence. He hewed great pillars from transcendent air. This is the sign: He saw, combined and brought forth all of creation from One Name. A sign of this is twenty-two objects in a single body.

The concept of bringing something from chaos, from "*tohu* and *bohu*," was first explored in Verse 1:11; here we are provided with additional detail about this process: God "hewed great pillars from transcendent air." These pillars may be visualized as the three pillars of the Tree of Life: the right or Male Pillar, the Pillar of Force; the left or Female Pillar, the Pillar of Form; and the Middle Pillar. These pillars form the structure of the universe. Transcendental air, the substance which God used to create these pillars, is the *Ruach of the Living God* from Verse 1:9. This *Ruach* was created from the *Ruach* of God, meaning the breath, spirit, will and desire of God.

The twenty-two letters are contained "in a single body"; which here refers to the Body of God, but which may also be seen as the body of Creation and, hence, on a lower level, the human body. Creation came from the One Name which, it is clear from the reference to the twenty-two objects, is the Hebrew alphabet.

The realization that our individual human bodies are part of the Body of God, and that our individual souls reside within the Soul of God, is the goal of much of Kabbalistic contemplation. Perle Epstein, in *Kabbalah: The Way of the Jewish Mystic*, speaks of 2nd century sage Rabbi Simeon bar Yochai: " 'All souls form but one unity with the Divine Soul,' was the basis for all his teachings. The entire aim of a man's stay on earth, said Rabbi Simeon, is to realize this in the experience of union:

All things of which this world is composed, as the soul and the body, will return to the principle and to the root from which they sprang. For God is the beginning and He is the end of all the degrees of creation. And all the degrees are bound with His seal. He is the unique Being, in spite of the innumerable forms in which He is clothed.

Rabbi Simeon's message is therefore a call to union with the Divine."[33]

As we shall see in later chapters, each one of the 22 letters is responsible for creating a particular aspect of the space-time universe and the human body. Contemplation of these letters is intended to heighten our awareness of the link between the twenty-two letters, our own bodies, our particular life experiences, and the world at large.

Suggestions for working with Verse 2:6

1. Contemplate the Verse for 15 minutes. Start by speaking the Verse aloud; then sit quietly, keeping the words in your mind. There is no need to memorize it; look at the text whenever you feel uncertain of the words.

2. Kabbalah teaches that each one of us is a microcosm of God. Visualize the Tree of Life's three pillars (shown in Figure 2, **Triangles and Pillars**) as massive, unimaginably enormous structures supporting the cosmos. In your mind's eye, watch these pillars shrink down to the size of the Milky Way, then down to the size of our solar system, then down to the size of the earth, and then down to the size of your own body: right side, left side and center. Know that we ourselves are the Tree of Life, a small version of an unimaginably large system, the microcosm of the macrocosm.

33 Epstein, Pearl. *Kabbalah: The Way of the Jewish Mystic.* Boston: Shambhala, 1988, p. 56.

Chapter Three
The Law of Three: *Aleph, Mem* and *Shin*

This Chapter describes the specific aspects of the physical world, time and humanity that emerge from the three mother letters.

Verse 3:1 Merit, Deficit and Balance

Three Mothers: Aleph Mem Shin. Their foundation is the scale of merit, the scale of deficit and the tongue balancing between them.

Verse 3:1 re-emphasizes Verse 2:1, reminding us that the three mother letters, *Aleph, Mem* and *Shin*, represent balance, merit, and deficit, respectively. This re-statement serves as a starting point for the remainder of the chapter, which describes the creative powers of the three mother letters in more detail.

As we learned in Verse 2:1, the Hebrew word for tongue is *lashon*. Its root word, *lash*, means "to knead" or "to combine different elements," which helps us understand that a place of balance does not comprise the absence of positive and negative, or of merit and deficit, but is actually composed of two such opposite forces well-blended together.

Suggestions for working with Verse 3:1 ═══════════

1. Write the Verse five times, slowly and deliberately. Contemplate each word as you write it.

2. Begin to chant "*Mem, Mem, Mem*". As you chant, bring in feelings of happiness, positivity, expansion and openness. Allow the chanting of "*Mem*" to make these feelings stronger. Then sit quietly and simply feel the energy of *Mem*. Then chant "*Shin, Shin, Shin*". As you chant, bring in feelings of sorrow, negativity, and restriction. The intent here is not to overwhelm yourself with such dark feelings, but to experience them in a controlled and safe environment. Allow the chanting of "*Shin*" to intensify these feelings, all the while remembering that you are completely safe. Then sit quietly and simply feel the energy of *Shin*. Finally, chant "*Aleph, Aleph, Aleph*" and bring in the experience of balance between *Mem* and *Shin*. Feel that you are large enough to encompass joy and sorrow, happiness and sadness, expansion and restriction in a way that does not compartmentalize these feelings but, instead, that allows them to mix and mingle with each other as part of your life, your day, and of each moment. Allow the chanting of *Aleph* to intensify your experience of encompassing these opposites. Then sit quietly and simply feel the energy of *Aleph*.

Verse 3:2 Mothers, Fathers and Descendants

Three Mothers: Aleph Mem Shin are a great secret, hidden and sealed in six rings; from which emerge air, fire and water, which split into male and female. The three mothers, Aleph Mem Shin, are the foundation; from them were born the fathers and descendants.

As expressed in Verse 3:1, the three mother letters created merit, deficit and balance. Verse 3:2 teaches us that the three mother letters also gave rise to air, fire and water, the six directions of physical space, and the concept of male and female energies. These six directions are the same six directions discussed in Verse 1:13, which God sealed with the six permutations of the letters *Yod Heh Vav*. Here, the six directions are envisioned not as points on a compass, but as six rings.

The three elements discussed in the *Sefer Yetzirah*, air, fire and water (rather than the four elements of the Aristotelian system or the five of the Chinese system), are a better fit for the Kabbalistic view of the universe, which is based on positive/negative/neutral or thesis/antithesis/resolution. Confusingly enough, however, Verse 6:1 states: "*These are the Three Mothers: Aleph Mem Shin. From them emanated Three Fathers, and they are air, water, and fire.*" Did the three elements actually emerge from Aleph Mem and Shin, or from a later emanation, called here "the fathers"? Rabbi and scholar Dr. Isidor Kalisch suggests that we should not understand the air, water and fire of Verse 3:2 as physical elements but as ethereal elements. "Here is meant: ethereal air, ethereal water, ethereal fire ..."[34] Ethereal elements have been conceptualized, but are not yet part of physical reality. We might think of these as Platonic elements.

The concept that creation emanates from the non-physical to the physical is basic to the Kabbalistic worldview. The mothers, fathers and descendants may be seen as moving down the Tree of Life. The mothers belong to the upper reaches of the Tree, where the energies of creation are

34 Kalisch, Rev. Dr. Isidor and Stenring, Knut. *Sepher Yetzirah: The Book of Creation.* San Diego, CA: The Book Tree, 2006, pg. 54.

gathered; the fathers belong to the mid-section of the Tree, where specific intentions are formulated; the descendants belong to the lower section of the Tree, where creation is expressed in the myriad forms of physical reality.

The three mother letters are referred to as a "great secret" because their true nature is hidden from the gaze of humankind. Further, the emergence of elements and directions from three letters is certainly not an easy or obvious concept. Our minds struggle with this idea and may even reject it. It's interesting to note that the word for universe is *Olam* (*Ayin Lamed Mem*), which also means "hiding." The origins and secrets of the universe hide from our eyes and our understanding.

Suggestions for working with Verse 3:2

1. Write the Verse five times, slowly and deliberately. Contemplate each word as you write it.

2. The Verse states "*Aleph Mem Shin are a great secret, hidden and sealed in six rings . . .*" Mankind has tried for millennium to understand how creation came about and how human consciousness originated. The Kabbalistic doctrine of emanation teaches us that the true origins of creation, the mothers, are hidden from view. The same is often true in the microcosm of our own lives. We think we understand something, but the truth is hidden. Consider what truths in your own life are hidden away.

Verse 3:3 Mother Letters in Space, Time and Humanity

Three mothers: He engraved them, hewed them, weighed them, interchanged them, combined them, and formed with them three mothers in the Universe, three mothers in the Year and three mothers in Humanity, male and female.

Again, we see that the six processes first described in Verse 2:2 (engraved, hewed, weighed, interchanged, combined, and formed) are employed in creation. These processes result in the five dimensions of height, depth, width, time, and spirituality, as introduced in Verse 1:5. Throughout the *Sefer Yetzirah*, the term "Universe" refers to the three dimensions of physical space; everything that is assigned to "Universe" exists in those dimensions. The term "Year" means the dimension of time; everything that is assigned to "Year" manifests as seasons, weeks, months or years.

The term "Humanity," however, is not quite as clear-cut as the other dimensions. The word used in the *Sefer Yetzirah* is *emesh*, which translates as both "body" and "soul." The interchangeability of body and soul is a key teaching of the *Sefer Yetzirah*. The dimension described in Verse 1:5 is spirituality or morality (depths of good and ill), but throughout the remainder of the text this dimension is expressed as a human body part and an aspect of the human life experience. The human body and life experience is thus linked to the dimension of good and ill.

At this point, many students struggle with the idea that spirituality is about humanity, and even more so with the idea of spirituality being tied to our physical bodies. This is a key teaching of the *Sefer Yetzirah*: the body is holy, humankind is holy; not sinful, not dirty, not ugly, but a perfect and consciously created reflection of God.

The *Sefer Yetzirah* views Time, Space and Humanity as alike in that all are created by the Hebrew letters. Time, Space and Humanity do have unique characteristics: the dimension of Time, unlike Space or Humanity, has cycles. The six dimensions of Space, unlike Time and Humanity, have a center. The dimension of Humanity, unlike Space and Time, contains contradictory impulses.

The use of the phrase "male and female", which occurs throughout the *Sefer Yetzirah*, does not refer to the possession of reproductive organs. The entire universe is seen as being either male (meaning an expansive, outward-directed energy) or female (meaning an enveloping, inward-directed energy). Even celestial bodies are viewed in this way: half the constellations in the visible sky (Gemini, Cancer, Virgo, Scorpio, Capricorn and Pisces) are considered female and the other half (Aries, Taurus, Leo, Libra, Sagittarius and Aquarius) are male. Among the seven ancient planets, three (Moon, Saturn and Venus) are considered female and the other four (Sun, Mars, Jupiter and Mercury) are male. The *Sefer Yetzirah* teaches us that the three mother letters created both male and female aspects and energies.

Suggestions for working with Verse 3:3

1. Consider male and female. Look around the room in which you are sitting. What do you see that might be considered male? A lamp, for example, may be thought of as male: it gives light and warmth. A drawer may be thought of as female: it receives and holds objects.

2. Each of us contains aspects of male and female. Contemplate your own male (giving) and female (receiving) aspects.

Verse 3:4 Mother Letters in Physical Space: Elements

*Three mothers: Aleph Mem Shin in the Universe: air, water, and fire.
Heaven was created from fire, earth was created from water and atmosphere was created from air, balancing the two.*

The next three Verses talk about the creative power of the three mother letters as they are manifested in the Universe (physical space), the Year (time) and Humanity (the human body).

Verse 3:4 shows the influence of the three mother letters in the Universe. We have already seen that *Aleph* is the tongue that balances between merit (*Mem*) and deficit (*Shin*), and that *Aleph* is visualized as the Middle Pillar balanced between the Female Pillar (*Shin*) and the Male Pillar (*Mem*). We have also seen that, through an intermediary called the fathers, air emanated from *Aleph*, water emanated from *Mem*, and fire emanated from *Shin*. This Verse takes us another step further in the creative process, explaining that heaven emanated from fire (which is *Shin*), earth emanated from water (*Mem*) and atmosphere emanated from air (*Aleph*).

As we shall see, all the Hebrew letters are assigned to paths on the Tree of Life; the three mother letters are assigned to the three horizontal paths. The top horizontal path on the Tree of Life is assigned to *Shin* which created heaven, the highest point; the lowest horizontal path is assigned to *Mem* which created earth, the lowest point; and the middle horizontal path is assigned to *Aleph* which created the atmosphere that separates earth from heaven. See Figure 10, **Mother Letters on the Tree**.

In our modern world fire is usually considered an active, "male" energy and water a passive, "female" energy. In Kabbalistic thinking, however, fire is a negative, destructive energy and thus female; water is a nourishing, positive energy and thus male. Contemporary students of Kabbalah are often troubled by this apparent reversal of the usual male and female attributes. The key to understanding this concept in the Kabbalistic sense is that birth, death and time are linked: when the archetypal female gives birth to form, she also gives birth to the end of form. The female energy is thus the bringer of both life and death.

Because air has no gender, it is energetically neutral. In the same way that neutrality separates positive and negative, so air separates fire and water, and atmosphere separates heaven and earth.

Suggestions for working with Verse 3:4

1. Write the Verse five times, slowly and deliberately. Contemplate each word as you write it.

2. The concept of gradual emanation is important in Kabbalah. We rarely appreciate the many small steps involved in the creative process. Select any creative process in which you participate—artwork, music, cooking, writing, decorating, even housecleaning—and consider how many stages there are between your decision to enter into that process and the end result. Consider too the many different "worlds" in which these stages manifest. Your will and desire play a part, as well as your critical thinking and judgment; you may experience a variety of emotions throughout, from excitement and anticipation to turmoil and disappointment; it is only later in the process that these different stages of experience bear fruit in physical creation. Select a creative activity you enjoy and see how many different steps you can identify; realize how difficult and complex this endeavor is and deeply appreciate yourself as a creator.

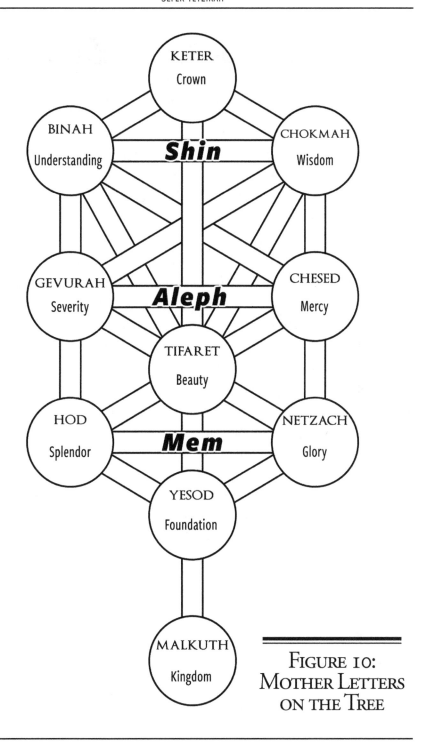

FIGURE 10:
MOTHER LETTERS
ON THE TREE

Verse 3:5 Mother Letters in Time: Seasons

Three mothers, Aleph Mem Shin, in the Year—hot, cold and temperate. Hot was created from fire, cold was created from water and temperate was created from air.

This Verse applies the creative energies of *Aleph*, *Mem* and *Shin* to the dimension of time as measured and symbolized by the Year. These three energies create the seasons of the year. While we divide our modern year into four seasons, the *Sefer Yetzirah* recognizes only three: hot, cold and temperate. The energies of *Aleph*, *Mem* and *Shin* cycle through the year: hot, of course, is summer, from the letter *Shin*, which also created fire; cold is winter, from the letter *Mem*, the source of water; temperate is both spring and fall, from the letter *Aleph*, which created air.

The word for temperate in the *Sefer Yetzirah* is *ravayah*. Friedman translates this word as "abundant"[35], which connotes notes food supplies and harvest, making this an apt term for both spring (the season in which food is planted) and fall (the season in which food is harvested). However, Glotzer translates *ravayah* as "saturated," meaning that the temperate season results from a complete saturation, or blending, of the two opposites.[36] We first encountered this concept of blending in Verse 3:1, where the word *lashon*, coming from the root word *lash*, was used to describe the "tongue" of *Aleph*. *Lash*, as we recall, means "to knead" or "to combine different elements." Again, we are taught that our place of balance derives not from an absence of positive and negative characteristics, but from a blending of these characteristics.

---

35 Friedman, Irving. *The Book of Creation.* New York, NY: Samuel Weiser, Inc., 1977, p. 7.

36 Glotzer, Leonard R. *The Fundamentals of Jewish Mysticism: The Book of Creation and Its Commentaries.* Northvale, NJ: Jason Aronson, Inc., 1992, p. 107.

Suggestions for working with Verse 3:5

1. Consider the season of the year and visualize the appropriate Hebrew letter. (See Table 1, **The Hebrew Letters**.) If it is winter, visualize *Mem*; if it is summer, *Shin*; if spring or fall, *Aleph*. Chant the letter softly. Visualize the letter moving, vibrating and spinning. As it spins, imagine it creating the characteristics of its season. *Mem* creates cold, snow, ice, frosty driveways and white meadows. *Shin* creates heat waves rising from the ground, scorched pavements, and sweat on our bodies. *Aleph* blends both hot and cold to create perfect spring and fall days, perfect for planting and harvesting. Spend some time watching the letter create the current season.

2. Note that a complete annual cycle includes two temperate seasons. Nature gives us a time to rest and regain our strength between the extremes of summer and winter. Consider that our lives also have seasons. We have seasons of tremendous power and growth; we have seasons of decay or hibernation; we have seasons in which very little seems to happen. Contemplate the events of your own life and see if you can identify your own cycle of seasons. What season are you in now? Are you able to appreciate that the cycling of seasons is a natural part of life?

Verse 3:6 Mother Letters in Humanity: Head, Chest and Belly

Three mothers, Aleph Mem Shin, in Humanity: head, chest and belly. The head was created from fire, the belly from water and the chest from air, which balances the two."

In this Verse, the three mother letters bring their creative energies into the dimension of Humanity. Because the energies of *Mem* created the element of water and is associated with depths (sea and land) in the dimension of the Universe, *Mem* is naturally assigned to a lower part of the human body: the belly. When we swallow food or drink, it goes to the belly. The energies of *Aleph* created the element of air. Since air divides heaven from earth, and spring and fall from winter and summer, it is naturally assigned to a mid-point in the human body: the chest. Air comes into our chest every time we breathe. The energies of *Shin* created the element of fire. Since it is associated with height (the heavens in the dimension of the Universe), it is naturally assigned to the topmost part of the human body: the head.

The *Sefer Yetzirah* teaches is that what appear to be very different things are simply diverse manifestations of one thing. For example, the human head, the season of summer and the element of fire are all *Shin* as expressed through the different dimensions of Universe, Year and Humanity. *Shin* links them all and is at their root.

This system of "correspondences," which link apparently unrelated objects via common roots, lies at the heart of the Western Magical Tradition. A great many of its traditional correspondences come directly from the *Sefer Yetzirah*.

These correspondences have been used throughout history for magical, meditative, and spiritual purposes. For example, it is often considered that rituals involving fire are best performed in the summer, when the energy of *Shin* is strongest. Chanting or writing the letter *Shin* gives that ritual increased power. Similarly, rituals or healing work aimed at the belly are best performed in winter, utilizing water and the letter *Mem*.

Suggestions for working with Verse 3:6

1. Close your eyes and feel the presence of the letter *Shin* on your forehead. *Shin* is fire; consider what aspects of your head are fire-like. Fire is the most energetic of the elements, and your head is the most energetic part of your body, receiving and processing more sensory impressions than any other organ, limb or system you possess. Expand your awareness to the rest of your body, and become aware that the warmth of the letter *Shin* is everywhere. With an internal temperature of 98.6 degrees, we are walking, talking, breathing furnaces, constantly emitting *Shin* by working, playing, thinking or simply living, and replenishing our supply of *Shin* by investing food and drink as fuel.

Now feel the presence of the letter *Aleph* on your chest. As you breathe in, the *Aleph* on your chest expands; as you breathe out, the *Aleph* on your chest shrinks. Realize that as you breathe in, you are inhaling a million tiny *Alephs*, which come rushing in through your nostrils, filling your lungs and your entire body. Appreciate these *Alephs* as life-bringers, giving you the gift of life with every breath you take. When you breathe out, picture a million tiny *Alephs* rushing out of your nostrils, re-joining the earth's atmosphere.

Now feel the presence of the letter *Mem* on your belly. As your awareness deepens, feel the presence of *Mem* inside your belly; then move your focus outward to encompass your entire body. Feel the omnipresence of *Mem*, of water, everywhere within you. We humans evolved from the sea, but we truly never left it. Our bodies are essentially sponges filled with water that we move with the help of appendage-sticks called bones. *Mem* is absolutely necessary for our survival. Throughout our day, we constantly take in *Mem* by eating and drinking and return *Mem* to the world through sweat and urine.

Verse 3:7 The Letter Aleph

He made the letter Aleph King over breath, crowned it, combined one with another, forming air in the World, the temperate of the Year, and the chest in Humanity, the male with Aleph Mem Shin and the female with Aleph Shin Mem.

Verse 3:8 The Letter Mem

He made the letter Mem King over Water, crowned it, and combined one with another, forming Earth in the World, cold in the Year, and belly in Humanity—the male with Mem Aleph Shin, and the female with Mem Shin Aleph.

Verse 3:9 The Letter Shin

He made the letter Shin King over Fire, crowned it, and combined one with another, forming the heavens in the World, heat in the Year, and the head in Humanity, the male with Shin Mem Aleph and the female with Shin Aleph Mem.

These Verses summarize many of the concepts regarding the mother letters that were introduced previously: *Aleph* formed the breath, air, temperate and the chest; *Mem* formed water, earth, cold and the human belly; *Shin* formed fire, the heavens, heat and the head.

The phrase "combined one with the other" means combining the letters *Aleph*, *Mem* and *Shin* to produce a certain result. The phrase "crowned it" means that each letter assumes a creative power similar to that of *Keter*, which translates as "crown." In Verse 3:7, *Aleph* is the crown and so it appears first in the letter combinations shown in that Verse: *Aleph Mem Shin* and *Aleph Shin Mem*. In Verse 3:8, *Mem* is the crown and so it appears first in the letter combinations shown in that Verse: *Mem Aleph Shin* and *Mem Shin Aleph*. In Verse 3:9, *Shin* is the crown and so it appears first in the letter combinations shown in that Verse: *Shin Aleph Mem* and *Shin Mem Alep*.

As we recall from Verse 2:4, changing the order of the letters reverses the meaning of the word; specifically, in these cases, from male to female. In the letter combination *Aleph Mem Shin*, the first letter and primary influence is *Aleph*; the second letter and secondary influence is *Mem*, the letter associated with the Male Pillar. This combination is thus considered male. In the letter combination *Aleph Shin Mem*, the first letter and primary influence is *Aleph*, associated with the neutral Middle Pillar; the second letter and secondary influence is *Shin*, the letter associated with the Female Pillar. Thus *Aleph Mem Shin* is a male combination and *Aleph Shin Mem* is a female combination.

Similarly, in the letter combinations *Mem Aleph Shin* and *Mem Shin Aleph*, the first letter and primary influence for both is *Mem*, the letter associated with the Male Pillar. However, the second letter and secondary influence of *Mem Aleph Shin* is *Aleph*, which is associated with the neutral Middle Pillar, while the second letter and secondary influence of *Mem Shin Aleph* is *Shin*, the letter associated with the Female Pillar. Thus, *Mem Shin Aleph* is considered female and *Mem Aleph Shin* is, by default, male.

Finally, in the letter combination *Shin Mem Aleph* and *Shin Aleph Mem*, the primary influence for both is *Shin*, the letter associated with the Female Pillar. However, the second letter and secondary influence of *Shin Mem Aleph* is *Mem*, which is assigned to the Male Pillar, while the second letter and secondary influence of *Shin Aleph Mem* is *Aleph*, the letter associated with the neutral Middle Pillar. Thus, *Shin Mem Aleph* is considered male and *Shin Aleph Mem* is, by default, female.

Here the *Sefer Yetzirah* is trying to prove its point from Verse 2:4: reversing the order of the letters reverses the meaning of the word. Verse 2:4 states: "*A sign for this is that there is nothing in good better than joy (Oneg: Ayin Nun Gimel) and there is nothing in evil worse than plague (Nega: Nun Gimel Ayin).*" This letter reversal works well in the example given: *Ayin Nun Gimel* means joy and *Nun Gimel Ayin* means plague. However, the concept doesn't work as well with the mother letters. We can almost make it work with the *Aleph* letter combinations. The meaning of the male three-letter combination *Aleph Mem Shin*, according to Matityahu Clark's *Etymological Dictionary of Biblical Hebrew*, is "to pass" or "to change." The meaning of the female three-letter root *Aleph Shin Mem* is more negative: it means "to destroy one's inner self" or "to self-destruct." Unfortunately, the other letter combinations do not yield similar results.

For modern students, it is perhaps more meaningful to note that the actual Hebrew word for "man" is *Aleph Yod Shin*, and the Hebrew word for "woman" is *Aleph Shin Heh*. Both start with the letter *Aleph*. Since *Aleph* is the meditating influence between fire and water, earth and heaven; men and women, both "crowned" with *Aleph*, serve as mediators between the spiritual and the material levels of Creation.

Table 3, **Mother Letter Correspondences**, summarizes what is created in the dimensions of Time, Space and Humanity by the mother letters.

TABLE 3: MOTHER LETTER CORRESPONDENCES

Letter	Shin	Aleph	Mem
Morality	Deficit	Balance	Merit
Path on the Tree	Chokmah-Binah	Chesed-Gevurah	Netzach-Hod
Macrocosm	Metaphysical Fire	Metaphysical Air	Metaphysical Water
Universe	Heavens	Atmosphere	Water/Earth
Elements	Terrestrial Fire	Terrestrial Air	Terrestrial Water/Earth
Human Body	Head	Chest	Belly
Year	Summer	Spring, Fall	Winter
Letter in the Tetragrammaton	Heh	Vav	Yod
Permutations Male/Female	ShAM/ShMA	AShM/AMSh	MShA/MASh

Suggestions for working with Verses 3:7-3:9 ===

1. The idea that we are mediators between heaven and earth is an important one in Kabbalah. This intermediary position places us, according to the Kabbalist, halfway between beast and angel. We have many of the traits of beasts: we have physical bodies, we eat flesh, we are often violent. We have many of the traits of angels: we have a soul, we are capable of self-sacrifice, we seek the Presence of God. But we have been given free will, which was given to neither beast nor angel. We do not have the option to become a beast or become an angel, but we can and do choose to move closer to one or the other. Consider your own position as an intermediary between beast and angel, and realize that your words and actions move you toward one or the other every minute of your life.

2. Experience the energies of *Aleph*, *Mem* and *Shin* more directly by meditating on the creative powers of the letters. Consult Table 1, **The Hebrew Letters**, to see what the letters look like. Contemplate *Aleph*, chant it softly, and envision the letter in your mind. Watch the letter as it begins to move and spin. As it spins, it takes on certain qualities: moderation, balance, silence. Note that *Aleph* is open, letting all the air in. As you watch in your mind's eye, air sweeps in from all directions, lifting the letter so it spins in the air. Watch as this air fills earth's atmosphere, protecting the earth and seas from the power of the sun.

Now contemplate *Mem*. Chant it softly and envision the letter in your mind. Watch Mem begin to move and spin; as it spins, it takes on certain qualities: wetness, coolness, the ability to reflect and the capacity take on the shape of whatever container holds it. Note that Mem has an opening at the bottom. As you watch, water begins to pour from that opening and fills the seas, lakes and rivers of Earth.

Finally, contemplate *Shin*. Chant it softly and envision the letter in your mind. Watch *Shin* begin to move and spin; as it spins, it takes on certain qualities: heat, movement, the ability to transform everything that it touches. Note that *Shin* looks like three flames. As you watch in your mind's eye, fire leaps up from the letter, rises to the skies and creates the sun, the stars and the heavens.

Chapter Four
The Law of Seven: *Bet, Gimel, Dalet, Kaf, Peh, Resh* and *Tav*

Chapter Four lists the seven double letters and describes what their creative power brings into the dimensions of Universe, Year and Humanity.

Verse 4:1 Seven Double Letters

Seven double letters, Bet, Gimel, Dalet, Kaf, Peh, Resh, Tav, are pronounced in two ways, symbolizing hard and soft, strong and weak.

The concept presented in this Verse is that each of these seven letters has a "hard" pronunciation and a "soft" pronunciation. An example of this dual pronunciation in English is the letter "C", which is sometimes pronounced as a hard "C" (as in the word "cat," where it sounds like the letter "K") and sometimes as a soft "C" (as in the word "cereal," where it sounds like the letter "S"). The two sets of pronunciations for *Bet, Gimel, Dalet, Kaf, Peh, Resh,* and *Tav* symbolize characteristics which can be hard or soft, strong or weak.

Many scholars believe that in ancient times there were two sets of pronunciations for all seven of these letters, but today's Hebrew recognizes different pronunciations only for four of them: *Bet, Kaf, Peh* and *Tav. Bet* is pronounced as both "B" and "V;" *Kaf* is pronounced as a hard "K" and as a guttural "Ch;" *Peh* is pronounced as both "P" and "F;" *Tav* is pronounced as both "T" and "S." The correct pronunciation of these four letters is designated by the presence or absence of a dot, called a *dagesh*, in the center of the letter. If the letter has a *dagesh*, it means the letter should be given the "hard" pronunciation; if the *dagesh* is absent, the letter is given the "soft" pronunciation.

Kaplan states that Yemenite Jews employ an alternate pronunciation of *Gimel* as a "J" sound, and an alternate pronunciation of *Dalet* as "Th."[37] It is possible that an alternate pronunciation of *Resh* once existed as a rolled "R", though Kalisch states that the alternate pronunciation of *Resh* is similar to the Greek letter *rho*.[38] For modern students, the pronunciation shown in Table 4, **Pronunciation of the Double Letters,** may be used for contemplation and magic.

TABLE 4: PRONUNCIATION OF THE DOUBLE LETTERS

Hebrew Character	Hard Pronunciation	Soft Pronunciation
ב	Bet	Vet
ג	Gimel	Jhimel
ד	Dalet	Thalet
כ	Kaf	Chaf*
פ	Peh	Feh
ר	Resh	Rresh (rolled r)
ת	Tav	Sav

*The "Ch" is a guttural sound in the back of the throat

37 Kaplan, Aryeh. *Sefer Yetzirah: The Book of Creation.* York Beach, ME: Samuel Weiser, Inc., 1997, p. 159.

38 Kalisch, Rev. Dr. Isidor and Stenring, Knut. *Sepher Yetzirah: The Book of Creation.* San Diego, CA: The Book Tree, 2006, p. 54.

Suggestions for working with this Verse:

1. Chant the Verse aloud several times. Start by speaking very slowly and softly; gradually get louder and faster, until finally your entire being is caught up in announcing these words to the world.

2. Consider the idea that the way in which you speak, i.e., the tone of your voice, may be as important as the words themselves. A sentence as simple as, "Oh, you look lovely," takes on a completely different meaning (in fact, the opposite meaning), when spoken in a sarcastic tone. Spend some time thinking about why it is that we allow our tone to convey a meaning that is different from the words themselves.

3. Reflect on the adjectives "soft" and "hard". What are your soft attributes? What are your hard attributes? Is soft always good? Is hard always bad?

Verse 4:2 Positive Attributes of the Seven Double Letters

*Seven double letters, Bet, Gimel, Dalet, Kaf, Peh, Resh, Tav symbolize
Wisdom, Wealth, Fertility, Life, Power, Peace and Beauty.*

These seven "soft" attributes are symbolized by "soft" pronunciation of the
letters of the letters *Bet, Gimel, Dalet, Kaf, Peh, Resh* and *Tav*. Wisdom is
associated with *Bet*, Wealth with *Gimel*, Fertility with *Dalet*, Life with *Kaf*,
Power with *Peh*, Peace withs *Resh* and Beauty with *Tav*.

Suggestions for working with this Verse:

1. Chant the seven Hebrew letters using the "soft" pronunciation from
Table 5, **Pronunciation of the Double Letters**. Do at least ten rounds of
the chant.

Verse 4:3 Negative Attributes of the Seven Double Letters

Seven double letters, Bet, Gimel, Dalet, Kaf, Peh, Resh, Tav. The opposite of Wisdom is Folly, the opposite of Wealth is Poverty, the opposite of Fertility is Barrenness, the opposite of Life is Death, the opposite of Power is Slavery, the opposite of Peace is War, and the opposite of Beauty is Ugliness.

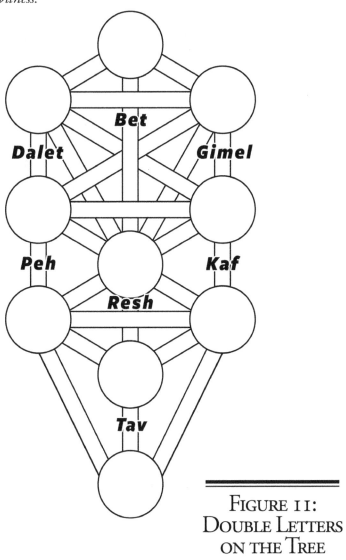

FIGURE 11:
DOUBLE LETTERS
ON THE TREE

The attributes assigned to the seven letters are human experiences that have opposites. The qualities listed in Verse 4:2 were entirely positive from the human viewpoint; these are entirely negative from that same view.

The seven opposites are represented on the Tree by the seven vertical paths. The *Sefer Yetzirah* does not tell us which letter is assigned to each path; different rabbis and teachers give different assignments. The letters seem to best fit our modern understanding of the Tree of Life when they are assigned as shown on Figure 11, **The Double Letters on the Tree**. *Kaf* symbolizes the qualities of life and death, and so is placed between *Chesed* and *Netzach* because *Netzach* represents life as manifested through the forces of nature. *Tav* symbolizes power and slavery, and so is placed between *Yesod* and *Malkuth*, as power is very much the concern of *Malkuth*.

The remaining letters—*Bet, Gimel, Dalet, Peh* and *Resh*—are assigned as follows. *Bet*, assigned to the qualities of wisdom and folly, is given the first of the vertical paths from *Keter* to *Tifaret*. *Gimel*, assigned to the qualities of wealth and poverty, is given the second position of *Chokmah* to *Chesed*. This is a good fit because wealth is a Jupiterian—and thus *Chesedic*—quality. *Dalet*, assigned to the qualities of fertility and barrenness, is placed on the path from *Binah* to *Gevurah*. This is appropriate because birth originates in *Binah*. *Peh*, assigned to the qualities of peace and war, is given to the path from *Gevurah*, the *Sephirah* of war, to *Hod*. *Resh*, assigned to the qualities of beauty and ugliness, is given to the path from *Tifaret* (meaning beauty) to *Yesod*.

Just as not all of us have equal amounts of merit (*Mem*), deficit (*Shin*) and balance (*Aleph*) in our characters, so not all of us have equal amounts of the negative and positive qualities represented by the double letters. Some people seem to have been blessed with a great deal of beauty, wealth or fertility; others spend their lives in poverty, are enslaved or are childless. Some people live in peace throughout their lives; others live in war-torn lands.

This imbalance on the individual level often feels unfair to us. We often blame our unhappiness on the lack of one or more of these attributes. Those of us who are not beautiful may feel that lack of beauty to be something that is wrong with us; those of us who do not enjoy material wealth may feel our poverty to be the cause of all our troubles; those of us who long for children feel that having children would make us perfectly happy.

The *Sefer Yetzirah* teaches us that both the negative and positive aspects are part of the Tree, and thus part of the Divine design. We may certainly attempt to correct what we feel to be a lack or inadequacy in our lives, while nonetheless recognizing that this lack is not wrong or evil.

It has been hypothesized that contemplating or chanting one pronunciation moves the practitioner toward one pole of the characteristic in question and contemplating or chanting the other pronunciation moves the practitioner in the other direction. In terms of the paths on the Tree, we may say that one pronunciation moves us upward toward *Keter*, while the other pronunciation moves us downward toward *Malkuth*. Kaplan states that the "hard" pronunciation moves us upward and the "soft" pronunciation moves us downward. However, he also quotes the *Tikkuney Zohar* as saying that the seven letters are like the *Chayot*, running and returning: "They run with the hard sound, and return with the soft."[39] This implies that the hard sound is linked to running away from God and thus down the Tree and the soft sound is linked to returning to God and thus up the Tree. The opinion of a number of modern aspirants involved in group work is that the soft sound moves the awareness upward, i.e., toward what we think of as the positive quality, and the hard sound moves the awareness downward, i.e., toward what we think of as the negative quality.

If, however, a student's experience yields a different result, that result should take precedence. The advanced student understands that the correct assignment of letters to path and attributes and the correct direction of hard and soft pronunciation is always that which works. Spiritual, magical, and contemplative practice is always pragmatic: it either works or it doesn't work.

---

39 Kaplan, Aryeh. *Sefer Yetzirah: The Book of Creation.* York Beach, ME: Samuel Weiser, Inc., 1997, p. 161.

It is important that we understand what this Verse is teaching us: the way in which we pronounce a letter does not change the basic creative energy of the letter, but it does change the way in which it manifests.

Suggestions for working with this Verse:

1. Chant the seven Hebrew letters using the "hard" pronunciation from Table 5, **Pronunciation of the Double Letters**. Do at least ten rounds of the chant.

Verse 4:4 Seven Directions

Seven double letters, Bet, Gimel, Dalet, Kaf, Peh, Resh, Tav, corresponding to the six directions, above, below, east, west, north, south and the holy palace in the center sustaining them all.

In Verse 1:13, we were told that God chose the three Mother letters, transposed *Aleph Mem Shin* into the letters *Vav Heh Yod* and created the six directions. In this Verse, the six directions are created again, but this time with the seven double letters. Why is another creation step necessary? It may be that the six directions created by *Vav Heh Yod* were Platonic directions, not yet actualized in the world; the six directions created with the seven double letters are now physical.

Also note that the six directions created by *Vav Heh Yod* did not have a center, while the six directions created by the seven double letters do have a center.

If the directions are given in order, then *Bet* is assigned to "above," *Gimel* to "below," *Dalet* to "east," *Kaf* to "west," *Peh* to "north," and *Resh* to "south." In that case, "the holy palace in the center" is assigned to *Tav*, the last letter of the Hebrew alphabet, which is symbolized on the Tree by the path in the center of the Tree between *Tiferet* and *Yesod*. See Figure 12, **Directions on the Tree**. These directions have also been assigned to faces of a cube, often called the Cube of Space, shown in Figure 13, **Cube of Space**. Some students find the Cube a useful device for contemplation, picturing themselves in the center. The three mother letters may be assigned to the three axes: *Aleph* is the above to below axis, *Mem* is side to side, and *Shin* is up to down.

Not everyone agrees, however, that the directions should be assigned to letters in the order given here. Aryeh Kaplan states that Rabbi Elijah ben Solomon assigned *Bet* to South, *Gimel* to North, *Dalet* to East, *Kaf* to Up, *Peh* to Down, *Resh* to West, and *Tav* to Center.[40] The phrase "the holy palace at the center" (*Hekhal HaKodesh* in Hebrew) refers to the indwelling

---

40 Kaplan, Aryeh. *Sefer Yetzirah: The Book of Creation.* York Beach, ME: Samuel Weiser, Inc., 1997, p. 164.

Presence of God within each of us. By stating that this Presence exists in the center, the *Sefer Yetzirah* teaches that when we are in a place of balance, when we have truly found our center, then we have found that Indwelling Presence. Finding the Presence that lives at our center and to live in constant awareness of that Presence is the work of the spiritual journey.

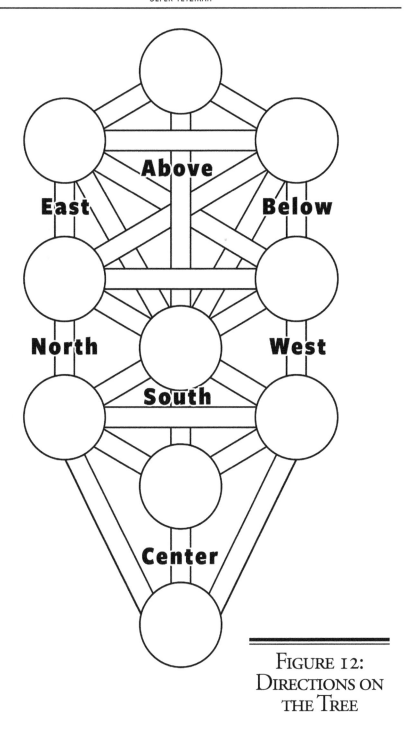

FIGURE 12:
DIRECTIONS ON
THE TREE

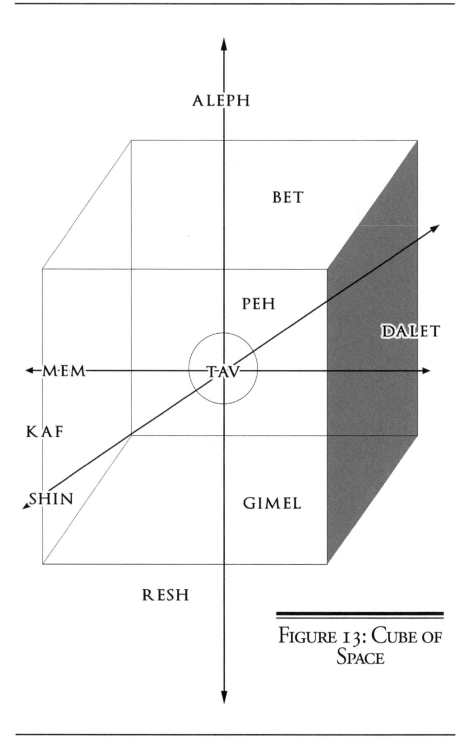

FIGURE 13: CUBE OF SPACE

Suggestions for working with this Verse:

1. Realize that each one of us has seven directions. Our directions of above and below are our head and our feet; our directions of north and south are our most "forward" point and our most "backward" point; our directions of east and south are our most "right-hand" point and our most "left-hand" point. And in the center of each of us in the Holy Palace, the Indwelling Presence of God and the place where we may communicate with the Divine. Stand quietly and send your awareness to your head; chant *Bet*. Then send your awareness to your feet and chant *Peh*. Move your awareness to the front of your body and chant *Gimel*. Move your awareness to the back of your body and chant *Resh*. Focus now on the right side of your body and chant *Dalet*. Focus on the left side of your body and chant *Kaf*. Finally, focus your attention on the very heart-center of your body and your inner being and chant *Tav*. Stand quietly for a few minutes, aware of all these directions of your own being and the Presence within.

Verse 4:5 Practice with the Double Letters

Seven double letters, Bet, Gimel, Dalet, Kaf, Peh, Resh, Tav, are seven and not six, seven and not eight. Contemplate/examine/study/ponder with them, establish them clearly and bring the Creator back to His Base.

Verse 1:4 used similar language in speaking of the ten *Sephirot*. As in that Verse, we are taught that by examining, contemplating, probing, searching, and pondering we bring God into our perception of the world. Similarly, by examining, contemplating, probing, searching, and pondering the seven double letters, we bring the various qualities and attributes of these letters into our perception of the world.

By so doing, we "seat the Creator on His base"; in other words, we come to understand God's place in the world and in our awareness. Kalisch's translation uses the phrase "make it so evident, that the Creator be acknowledged to be on His throne again," indicating that such studies make God's presence evident to the student.[41]

The many verbs used in this Verse to describe how we work with the letters suggest the depth to which we must apply ourselves in this work. Most of us have an eclectic assortment of spiritual techniques: we chant, we pray, we study, we contemplate, we work on our character, we attend retreats, on and on, twisting and turning, this way and that. We create an entire toolbox of practices and are on the lookout for new ones all the time. This Verse reminds us that whatever we choose to do, we must do it deeply, with all our heart and soul, if we are to "bring the Creator back to His Base."

---

41 Kalisch, Rev. Dr. Isidor and Stenring, Knut. *Sepher Yetzirah: The Book of Creation.* San Diego, CA: The Book Tree, 2006, p. 30.

Suggestions for working with this Verse:

1. It is easy for us to become distracted by the many activities of our lives. We give our attention to our possessions, our money, our relationships and our bodies. Days, weeks and years can pass without our attention moving up to the spiritual world. Contemplate the actions we take to become aware of God and our own spirituality. Evaluate the depth of your commitment to these practices.

Verse 4:6 Double Letters in Space, Time and Humanity

Seven double letters, Bet, Gimel, Dalet, Kaf, Peh, Resh, Tav. He engraved them, hewed them, weighed them, interchanged them, combined them, and formed with them the seven planets in the Universe, seven days in the Year and seven gateways in Humanity, male and female.

This Verse parallels Verse 2:2, which explained the process by which the twenty-two letters were expressed in the five dimensions of space (Universe), time (Year) and spirituality (Humanity), and Verse 3:3, which explained the process by which the three mother letters were expressed in those five dimensions. This Verse does the same for the seven double letters. Through the various processes of engraving, hewing, weighing, interchanging and combining, the seven planets, seven days of the week and seven openings in the head are formed.

Suggestions for working with this Verse:

1. Consider the differences in the way we interact with the universe, year and soul. We have some amount of free will in moving through the physical universe and technology gives us even more of that free will. However, we have no free will in moving through the dimension of time. We cannot move faster or more slowly through time. Do we have free will in moving through the dimension of spirituality? What limits our free will in that dimension?

Verse 4:7 Seven Planets, Days and Gateways

Seven planets in the Universe: Saturn, Jupiter, Mars, Sun, Venus, Mercury, Moon. Seven days in the Year: the seven days of the week. Seven gateways in Humanity: two eyes, two ears, two nostrils, and the mouth.

This Verse provides the names of the seven planets, days of the week and openings in the head.

The seven planets named here are often called the "seven ancient planets." Only Saturn, Jupiter, Mars, Venus and Mercury are actually planets, but the ancient world believed that the Sun and Moon also circled the earth. The order of the planets in this system, known as the Ptolemaic system, is Moon, Mercury, Venus, Sun, Mars, Jupiter and Saturn. The order given in many of the translations of the *Sefer Yetzirah* is the Ptolemaic order, starting with the farthest (Saturn) and ending with the closest (Moon). Kalisch says that the order used in earlier translations of the *Sefer Yetzirah* is Mars, Jupiter, Saturn, Moon, Mercury, Venus, Sun.[42]

The planets are believed to exert both positive and negative influences on mankind, continuing the double letter theme of "opposites." There is no agreement as to the assignment of planets to letters; *Sefer Yetzirah: Magic and Mysticism*, assigns planets based on the attributes of the letters. Thus, *Gimel*, assigned to the qualities of wealth and poverty, is assigned to Jupiter, the planet of material wealth. *Dalet*, assigned to fertility and barrenness, is assigned to the Moon, which controls the female fertility cycle. *Kaf*, assigned to life and death, is assigned to Saturn, the planet of mortality. *Peh*, assigned to peace and war, is assigned to Mars, the planet of war. *Resh*, assigned to beauty and ugliness, is assigned to Venus, the planet of physical beauty. *Tav*, assigned to power and slavery, is assigned to the Sun, the most powerful of the seven ancient planets.

Jewish tradition assigns an angel to each of the planets. The angel's job is to channel the power of the letter from the higher worlds to the

42 Kalisch, Rev. Dr. Isidor and Stenring, Knut. *Sepher Yetzirah: The Book of Creation.* San Diego, CA: The Book Tree, 2006, p. 55.

lower worlds. Tradition teaches that there are two different kinds of angels. Temporary angels do not have names or physical bodies; they have a very specific mission and cease to exist as soon as that mission is completed. Permanent angels have more enduring missions, and possess names and bodies. Their bodies are the planets and stars; as our bodies are focal points for our souls, so the planets are focal points for the angels.

There is no traditional agreement as to how angels are assigned to planets. Kaplan provides a table of different assignments of angel to planet, showing that Michael or Kaptziel are generally assigned to Saturn; Berakiel, Tzidkiel or Raphael to Jupiter; Gabriel or Samael to Mars; Raphael or Michael to the Sun; Chasdiel, Tzidkiel or Anel to Venus; Tzidkiel, Chasdiel, Raphael, Barakiel or Michael to Mercury; and Anel or Gabriel to the Moon.[43] *The Book of the Angel Reziel*, as translated by Steve Sadow, assigns Michael to Saturn, Bereqial to Jupiter, Gabriel to Mars, Dodenial to the Sun, Chesedial to Venus, Tzedeqial to Mercury, and A'aniel to the Moon.[44] *The Greater Key of Solomon* assigns Saturn to Cassiel, Jupiter to Sachiel, Mars to Zamael, the Sun to Michael, Venus to Anael, Mercury to Raphael and the Moon to Gabriel.[45]

Sefer Yetzirah: Magic and Mysticism assigns Saturn to Kaptziel, Jupiter to Barakiel, Mars to Michael, the Sun to Raphael, Venus to Gabriel, Tzidkiel to Mercury and Chasdiel to the Moon, based on contemplation and experimentation.

It is interesting that the planets and openings are named in this Verse, but the days of the week are not. This is because the only day of the week that actually has a name in Hebrew is the Sabbath, called, in Hebrew, *Shabbat*. The other names of days are simply First Day (*Yom Rishon*), Second Day (*Yom Sheini*), Third Day (*Yom Shlishi*), Fourth Day (*Yom R'vi'i*), Fifth Day (*Yom Chamishi*), and Sixth Day (*Yom Shishi*). The names of the week that are in common use today come from the Romans: Sunday was sacred to the Sun; Monday to the

43 Kaplan, Aryeh. *Sefer Yetzirah: The Book of Creation.* York Beach, ME: Samuel Weiser, Inc., 1997, p. 168.

44 Sadow, Steve. *Book of the Angel Rezial.* San Francisco, CA: Weiser Books, 2006, pp. 119–120.

45 Mathers, S. Liddell MacGregor. *The Greater Key of Solomon.* ILL: De Laurence, Scott and Co., 1914, p. 7.

moon; Tuesday to Tiw, a war god; Wednesday to Woden, the leader of the gods; Thursday to Thor, the god of thunder; Friday to Frigge, the wife of Woden; and Saturday to Saturn, god of crops and harvest. Needless to say, Judaism does not favor naming days after pagan gods.

The seven "gateways" are the seven openings in the head: the two eyes, two nostrils, two ears and mouth. These are our "gateways" to the outside world, allowing us to take in the information we need to survive.

There is no agreement as to the assignment of letters to head openings; the *Sefer Yetzirah: Magic and Mysticism* assigns the seven vertical paths of the Tree to the openings in the head in a manner that most closely duplicates a face. The two nostrils and the mouth are assigned to the three paths in the center of the Tree. The left ear and left eye are assigned to the two vertical paths on the left side of the Tree (from the Tree's perspective, not the viewer's perspective). The right ear and right eye are assigned to the two vertical paths on the right side of the Tree. See Figure 14, **Seven Openings on the Tree**.

The *Sefer Yetzirah* considers the human body to be a mirror of the human soul. That means that these seven "gateways" or avenues of information from the physical world have a parallel in the spiritual world. Many of us can "see," "hear" and "smell" auras, voices and odors in the non-physical world. Further, many of us are able to speak, silently, in the non-physical world. Silent prayer is an example of this.

Suggestions for working with this Verse:

1. Consider your own level of development in the non-physical realms. Are you aware of taking in information on that level? In what ways does this information become available to you?

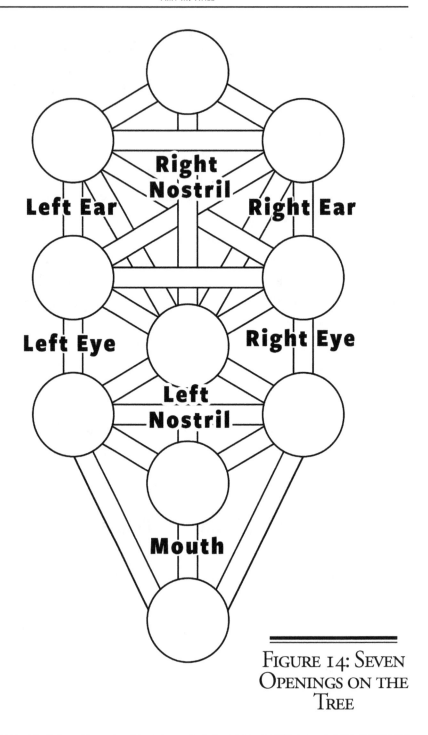

FIGURE 14: SEVEN OPENINGS ON THE TREE

Verse 4:8 The Letter Bet

He made the letter Bet king over Wisdom, bound a crown to it, combined one with another; and with them He formed the Mercury in the Universe, the first day in the Year, and the right nostril in Humanity, male and female.

The letter *Bet* is assigned to the qualities of wisdom and folly, and the planet Mercury. It is assigned to the first day, Sunday, and the right nostril. The angel Tzidkiel is assigned to Mercury.

Suggestions for working with this Verse:

1. Perform the following contemplation on a Sunday. Because the letter *Bet* is associated with the number 2, a Sunday with a date of 2, 11 or 20 is ideal. Contemplate the letter *Bet*. Let *Bet* fill your vision and your mind. Picture *Bet* coming down from the spiritual realms, assisted by the angel Tzidkiel, forming the planet Mercury in the three dimensions of space, forming Sunday in the dimension of time, forming the right nostril in your own body and the qualities of wisdom and folly in your life experience. Consider how these qualities manifest in your life today. In what ways have you been wise? When have you engaged in folly? What differentiates wisdom from folly?

Verse 4:9 The Letter Gimel

He made the letter Gimel king over Wealth, bound a crown to it, combined one with another; and with them He formed Jupiter in the Universe, the second day in the Year, and the right ear in Humanity, male and female.

The letter *Gimel* is assigned to the qualities of wealth and poverty and the planet Jupiter, which is associated with material wealth. It is assigned to the second day, Monday, and the right ear. The angel Barakiel is assigned to Jupiter.

Suggestions for working with this Verse:

1. Perform the following contemplation on a Monday. Because the letter *Gimel* is associated with the number 3, a Monday with a date of 3, 12, 21 or 30 is ideal. Contemplate the letter *Gimel*. Let *Gimel* fill your vision and your mind. Picture *Gimel* coming down from the spiritual realms, assisted by the angel Barakiel, forming the planet Jupiter in the three dimensions of space, forming Monday in the dimension of time, forming the right ear in your own body and the qualities of wealth and poverty in your life experience. Consider how these qualities manifest in your life today. Look more deeply than just your financial situation: in what other ways does wealth and poverty manifest? We may be poor in pocket, but wealthy in many other ways; or vice versa.

Verse 4:10 The Letter Dalet

He made the letter Dalet king over Fertility, bound a crown to it, combined one with another; and with them He formed the Moon in the Universe, the third day in the Year, and the left ear in Humanity, male and female.

The letter *Dalet* is assigned to the qualities of fertility and barrenness, and the Moon, which is associated with the female fertility cycle. It is assigned to the third day, Tuesday, and the left ear. The angel Chasdiel is assigned to the Moon.

Suggestions for working with this Verse:

1. Perform the following contemplation on a Tuesday. Because the letter *Dalet* is associated with the number 4, a Tuesday with a date of 4, 13, 22 or 31 is ideal. Contemplate the letter *Dalet*. Let *Dalet* fill your vision and your mind. Picture *Dalet* coming down from the spiritual realms, assisted by the angel Chasdiel, forming the Moon in the three dimensions of space, forming Tuesday in the dimension of time, forming the left ear in your own body and the qualities of life and death in your life experience. Consider how these qualities manifest in your life today.

2. *Gimel* and *Dalet* are assigned to the ear. We can use these letters to develop our ability to hear in the physical world and in subtler realms as well. Chant "*Gimel, Dalet*" repeatedly aloud, gradually reducing the volume to a whisper, then chanting silently in the mind. Then let silence fill your mind. Listen for soft sounds that are almost unnoticeable—the sound of the clock ticking, the house creaking, your own rhythmic breathing. Then listen for things that are still quieter: the presence of others in the house, the hum of their thoughts and life processes. And on an even subtler level, listen for the sound of the Presence in the world. As you gain proficiency, you can use the *Gimel, Dalet* chant whenever you need to hear more deeply or more truthfully.

Verse 4:11 The Letter Kaf

He made the letter Kaf king over Life, bound a crown to it, combined one with another; and with them He formed Saturn in the Universe, the fourth day in the Year, and the right eye in Humanity, male and female.

The letter *Kaf* is assigned to the characteristics of Life and Death, and the planet Saturn, which is traditionally associated with death. It is assigned to the fourth day, Wednesday, and the right eye. The angel Kaptziel is assigned to Saturn.

Suggestions for working with this Verse:

1. Perform the following contemplation on a Wednesday. Because the letter *Kaf* is associated with the number 20, a Wednesday with a date of 2, 11, or 20 is ideal. Contemplate the letter *Kaf*. Let *Kaf* fill your vision and your mind. Picture *Kaf* coming down from the spiritual realms, assisted by the angel Kaptziel, forming the planet Saturn in the three dimensions of space, forming Wednesday in the dimension of time, forming the right eye in your own body and the qualities of life and death in your life experience. Consider how these qualities manifest in your life today. What part of your being is particularly alive right now? What is approaching death? These cycles are a natural part of the rhythms of our lives.

Verse 4:12 The Letter Peh

He made the letter Peh king over Peace, bound a crown to it, combined one with another; and with them He formed Mars in the Universe, the fifth day in the Year, and the left eye in Humanity, male and female.

The letter *Peh* is assigned to the characteristics of peace and war, and to Mars, which is associated with warfare. It is assigned to the fifth day, Thursday, and the left eye. The angel Michael is assigned to Mars.

Suggestions for working with this Verse:

1. Perform the following contemplation on a Thursday. Because the letter *Peh* is associated with the number 80, a Thursday with a date of 8, 17 or 26. Contemplate the letter *Peh*. Let *Peh* fill your vision and your mind. Picture *Peh* coming down from the spiritual realms, assisted by the angel Michael, forming Mars in the three dimensions of space, forming Thursday in the dimension of time, forming the left eye in your own body and the qualities of peace and war in your life experience. Consider how these qualities manifest in your life today. In what areas of your life do you experience peace? In what areas do you feel that you are at war?

2. *Kaf* and *Peh* are assigned to the eyes. We can use these letters to develop our ability to see in the physical world and in subtler realms as well. Select an object to look at: a candle, flame, rock, photograph. Chant *"Kaf, Peh"* repeatedly aloud, gradually reducing the volume to a whisper, then chanting silently in the mind. Then let silence fill your mind and gaze at the object you've selected. Observe the obvious physical characteristics: shape, size, color, etc. Deepen your gaze until you begin to see subtler attributes and textures, curves and straight lines. Deepen your gaze again, now looking at the material from which the object was made. Look even more deeply, until you see that the object consists mainly of empty space and vibratory energy. Use this chant whenever you need to see more deeply into the truth of something in your life.

Verse 4:13 The Letter Resh

He made the letter Resh king over Beauty, bound a crown to it, combined one with another; and with them He formed Mars in the Universe, the sixth day in the Year, and the left nostril in Humanity, male and female.

The letter *Resh* is assigned to the qualities of beauty and ugliness, and the planet Venus, traditionally associated with beauty. It is assigned to the sixth day, Friday, and the left nostril. The angel Gabriel is assigned to Venus.

Suggestions for working with this Verse:

1. Perform the following contemplation on a Friday. Because the letter *Resh* is associated with the number 200, a Friday with a date of 2, 11 or 20 is ideal. Contemplate the letter *Resh*. Let *Resh* fill your vision and your mind. Picture *Resh* coming down from the spiritual realms, assisted by the angel Gabriel, forming the planet Venus in the three dimensions of space, forming Friday in the dimension of time, forming the left nostril in your own body and the qualities of beauty and ugliness in your life experience. Consider how these qualities manifest in your life today. What is beautiful in your world today? What ugliness is there? Is ugliness always bad?

Verse 4:14 The Letter Tav

He made the letter Tav king over Power, bound a crown to it, combined one with another; and with them He formed the Sun in the Universe, the Sabbath in the Year, and the mouth in Humanity, male and female.

The letter *Tav* is assigned to the qualities of power and slavery, and to the Sun, the most powerful of the seven ancient planets. It is assigned to the seventh day, Saturday, and the mouth. The angel Raphael is assigned to the Sun.

See Table 5, **Double Letter Correspondences**, for a summary of the double letter correspondences.

Suggestions for working with this Verse:

1. Perform the following contemplation on a Saturday. Because the letter *Tav* is associated with the number 400, a Saturday with a date of 4, 13, 22 or 31 is ideal. Contemplate the letter *Tav*. Let *Tav* fill your vision and your mind. Picture *Tav* coming down from the spiritual realms, forming the Sun in the three dimensions of space, assisted by the angel Raphael, forming Saturday in the dimension of time, forming the mouth in your own body and the qualities of beauty and ugliness in your life experience. Consider how these qualities manifest in your life today. What power have you gained in your life? Is there still something that enslaves you?

2. *Tav* is assigned to the mouth. We can use *Tav* to develop our ability to speak more truthfully. Chant *Tav* repeatedly aloud, gradually reducing the volume to a whisper, then chanting silently in the mind. Then let silence fill your mind. Consider something you've said in the past few days; then consider what might have been a more truthful statement or approach. Repeat the chant, and find an even deeper truth.

Table 5: Double Letter Correspondences

Letter	Qualities	Direction	Planet	Day	Body	Path	Angel
Bet	Wisdom/ Folly	Above	Mercury	Sunday	Rt. nostril	Keter-Tifaret	Tzidkiel
Gimel	Wealth/ Poverty	Below	Jupiter	Monday	Rt. eye	Chokmah-Chesed	Barakiel
Dalet	Fertility/ Barrenness	East	Moon	Tuesday	Lt. eye	Binah-Gevurah	Chasdiel
Kaf	Life/ Death	West	Saturn	Wednesday	Rt. ear	Chesed-Netzach	Kaptziel
Peh	Peace/War	North	Mars	Thursday	Lt. ear	Gevurah-Hod	Micahel
Resh	Beauty/ Ugliness	South	Venus	Friday	Lt. nostril	Tifaret-Yesod	Gabriel
Tav	Power/ Slavery	Center	Sun	Saturday	Mouth	Yesod-Malkuth	Raphael

Verse 4:15 He Loves Sevens

Seven double letters—Bet, Gimel, Dalet, Kaf, Peh, Resh, Tav—with them were engraved seven worlds, seven heavens, seven lands, seven seas, seven rivers, seven deserts, seven days, seven weeks, seven years, seven sabbaticals, seven jubilees, and the Holy Palace. He loves all sevens in everything under the heavens.

There are indeed a lot of sevens in our world. There are seven layers of skin, the rainbow has seven colors, the octave has seven notes, the seven son has special power, there are seven deadly sins, seven wonders of the Ancient World, Jewish brides walk seven circles around their grooms. Seven is a sepcial number in dice. A week contains seven days in almost every culture, for reasons unknown, as there is no astronomical reason for this to occur. In the Rig Vega, Sanskirt's holy ancient book, there are seven stars, seven concentric continents, and seven streams of soma, the drink of the gods. The Egyptians described seven paths to heaven. On and on, the number seven has a special place in the world. Here is Glotzer's view:

"I believe the unique quality of these numbers is due to three factors:

1. They add up to ten.
2. They are prime numbers.
3. They are different from one another.

"If ten is broken into two numbers whose sum is ten, five pairs are possible: 1 and 9, 2 and 8, 3 and 7, 4 and 6, and 5 and 5. Each pair except (3 and 7) and (5 and 5) have elements that can be divided by a number other than themselves or one. For instance, 9 can be expressed as 3 x 3 and thus is not prime. The pair 5 and 5 is redundant and does not produce two separate numbers. Thus 3 and 7 are special."[46]

46 Glotzer, Leonard R. *The Fundamentals of Jewish Mysticism: The Book of Creation and Its Commentaries.* Northvale, NJ: Jason Aronson, Inc., 1992, p. 122.

Prime numbers are spiritually significant because they are divisible only by themselves and 1; thus, they represent God, the Prime Mover and Original Source. Like prime numbers, God cannot be reduced to something smaller. The importance of the number 10, as mentioned in the Introduction, is that the ancient Hebrew numbering system called Prat Katan regards the number 10 as being the same as the number 1. The numbers 3 and 7, which are the only two unique prime numbers that add up to 10, thus become the building blocks of multiplicity.

The seven worlds are the seven planets, as discussed earlier. Seven firmaments are the seven heavens, mentioned in the Tractate of Hagigah in the Talmud. They are *Vilon* (meaning "curtain"), *Rakia* (meaning "firmament"), *Shehakim* (meaning "skies"), *Zevul* (meaning "habitation"), *Ma'on* (another word for "habitation"), *Makhon* (and yet another word for "habitation") and *Aravot* (meaning "clouds"). The idea of seven heavens came from Babylonian astronomy and early Greek science, which hypothesized that each of the seven planets inhabited a zone, or heaven, of its own. It is interesting that today scientists recognize seven layers of the Earth's atmosphere: troposphere, stratosphere, mesosphere, thermosphere, exosphere, isonosphere and magnetosphere.

The idea of ascending up through various layers, or heavens, was part of a branch of Jewish mysticism called *Hekhalot*, or "Chariot," mysticism. *Hekhalot* mysticism required the mystic to ascend through the seven heavens, overcoming various challenges, then pass through seven palaces in the seventh heaven in order to reach God's throne. "Seventh heaven" came to mean "bliss." The idea also exists in Islam; we read in Sura 71 of the *Quran*: "See you not how Allah has created the seven heavens one above another, and made a moon a light in their midst and made the sun a lamp?"

The seven lands are *Adamay, Tevel, Nashiyah, Tzaya, Chalad, Eretz* and *Chalad*, or possibly *Adamah, Tevel, Nasya, Tzaya, Eretz, Arkah* and *Gey*. In modern terms, we may think of the seven lands as the seven continents: Africa, Antarctica, Asia, Australia. Europe, North America, and South America.

The seven seas referenced here may be Tiberias, Socom, Chaylot, Chulte, Sivchay, Spain and the Great Sea. There are over 50 seas known today, but the term "seven seas" is an old one, appearing as early as 2300 BCE in Hymn 8 of the Sumerian Enheduanna to the goddess Inanna.

The seven rivers are Jordan, Yarmoch, Kirmyon, Poga, Pishon, Gichon and Chidekel (or the Euphrates). The seven deserts are those which the Israelites passed through during the Exodus: Eitan, Shur, Sin, Sinai, Paran, Tzin and Kadmut.

The seven days are the seven days of the week; seven weeks are the weeks between the Jewish holidays of Pesach and Shavuot. The seven years are a reference to the sabbatical cycle. Leviticus 25:3–4: "Six years you may sow your field, and six years you may prune your vineyard and gather the produce, but in the seventh year the land must have a Sabbath of complete rest—a Sabbath to the LORD. You must not sow your field or prune your vineyard." The concept of the sabbatical year may apply to millennia. Sanhedrin 97a says: "R. Kattina said, Six thousand years shall the world exist, and one thousand it shall lay desolate." (The year 2010 is equivalent to the Jewish year 5770–5771, leaving roughly 230 years before desolation.) Another school of thought is that one divine day is equal to a thousand years; this school references Psalms 90:4: "A thousand years in Your sight are as but yesterday." In that case, 7000 divine years = 2,556,750,000 earth years. Modern science confirms that life has existed on this planet for approximately two billion years.

Seven sabbaticals refer to the Jubilee year, which is the year after seven sabbatical cycles. The Jubilee year occurs every 50 years. During the Jubilee year, all slaves go free and property is returned to its hereditary owner. Seven Jubilees is thus seven times 50 or 350 years.

Other important uses of the number seven: Passover and Sukkot are seven days long; the seventh month is the month of the New Year; there are seven festivals during which no work may be done: Rosh Hashanah, Yom Kippur, 1st day of Sukkot, Shemini Atzeret, 1st and 7th days of Passover, Shavuot; there are seven candles in a menorah; there are seven notes in the diatonic musical scale. There is a tradition that there are seven names of God that require a scribe to take special care: Eloah, Elohim, Adonai, Ehyeh-Asher-Ehyeh, YHVH, Shaddai and Tzevaoth. There are seven colors in the rainbow.

The reference to the Holy Palace may remind us that God is at the center of everything. It may also refer to the idea that the number seven consists of three things on one side, three things on the other side, and one thing in the center. We may think of this as the three *sephirot* of the Male pillar (*Chokmah, Chesed* and *Netzach*), the three *sephirot* of the Female pillar (*Binah, Gevurah* and *Hod*) and the middle pillar as the center.

Suggestions for working with this Verse:

1. We know today that most of the universe is actually empty space; it is our human minds that create patterns. We connect the dots, as it were, to create the images of constellations in the night sky, the image of man as a reflection of God, and all the various stories of our lives. If we look for sevens, we find them. How are you connecting the dots to form the patterns, the stories, in your own life? How might the dots be connected differently?

Verse 4:16 Building Houses with Stones

Two stones build 2 houses, three stones build 6 houses, four stones build 24 houses, five stones build 120 houses, six stones build 620 houses, seven stones build 5040 houses; from here on, figure that which the mouth cannot speak and the ear cannot hear.

Stones are letters; houses are words. The use of "building" as an analogy is a common one in western mysticism. God is often referred to as the Master Builder or the Architect of the Universe. Also, in the Masonic tradition, Hiram Abiff was the Master Builder of King Solomon's Temple; he knew many important secrets, one of which was the name of God (called the "Grand Masonic Word").

From two letters, we get two words. For example, the two letters *Bet* and *Gimel* produce *Bet Gimel* and *Gimel Bet*. From three letters, we get six words. The mathematical formula for this type of calculation is called a "factorial." Three factorial (abbreviated as 3!) = 3x2 = 6. Four factorial (abbreviated as 4!) = 4x3x2 = 24. Five factorial or 5! = 5x4x3x2 = 120. Six factorial or 6! = 6x5x4x3x2 = 720. Seven factorial or 7! = 6x5x4x3x2 = 5040.

The statement that "the mouth is unable to utter and the ear cannot hear" refers to the practice of chanting these letter permutations. It takes about 15 seconds to "build" 6 "houses, or chant the six permutations, in Exercise 2 below. Exercise 3, in which we chant 24 four-letter permutations takes just over a minute. Exercise 4, in which we chant 120 five-letter permutations takes about 6 ½ minutes. Exercise 5, with its 720 six-letter permutations takes about 45 minutes. Chanting 5040 seven-letter permutations would take about seven hours. And if we were to chant the 40,320 eight-letter permutations, it would take well over two days – certainly more than the mouth can speak or the ear can hear.

Suggestions for working with this Verse:

1. Build 2 houses. Chant *Bet Gimel* and *Gimel Bet* several times.

2. Build 6 houses. Chant:

> *Bet Gimel Dalet*
> *Bet Dalet Gimel*
> *Gimel Bet Dalet*
> *Gimel Dalet Bet*
> *Dalet Bet Gimel*
> *Dalet Gimel Bet*

3. Build 24 houses. Chant:

> *Bet Gimel Dalet Kaf*
> *Bet Gimel Kaf Dalet*
> *Bet Kaf Gimel Dalet*
> *Kaf Bet Gimel Dalet*
> *Bet Dalet Gimel Kaf*
> *Bet Dalet Kaf Gimel*
> *Bet Kaf Dalet Gimel*
> *Kaf Bet Dalet Gimel*
> *Gimel Bet Dalet Kaf*
> *Gimel Bet Kaf Dalet*
> *Gimel Kaf Bet Dalet*
> *Kaf Gimel Bet Dalet*
> *Gimel Dalet Bet Kaf*
> *Gimel Dalet Kaf Bet*
> *Gimel Kaf Dalet Bet*
> *Kaf Gimel Dalet Bet*
> *Dalet Bet Gimel Kaf*
> *Dalet Bet Kaf Gimel*
> *Dalet Kaf Bet Gimel*

Kaf Dalet Bet Gimel
Dalet Gimel Bet Kaf
Dalet Gimel Kaf Bet
Dalet Kaf Gimel Bet
Kaf Dalet Gimel Bet

4. Build 120 houses

Bet Gimel Dalet Kaf Peh
Bet Gimel Dalet Peh Kaf
Bet Gimel Peh Dalet Kaf
Bet Peh Gimel Dalet Kaf
Peh Bet Gimel Dalet Kaf

Bet Gimel Kaf Dalet Peh
Bet Gimel Kaf Peh Dalet
Bet Gimel Peh Kaf Dalet
Bet Peh Gimel Kaf Dalet
Peh Bet Gimel Kaf Dalet

Bet Kaf Gimel Dalet Peh
Bet Kaf Gimel Peh Dalet
Bet Kaf Peh Gimel Dalet
Bet Peh Kaf Gimel Dalet
Peh Bet Kaf Gimel Dalet

Kaf Bet Gimel Dalet Peh
Kaf Bet Gimel Peh Dalet
Kaf Bet Peh Gimel Dalet
Kaf Peh Bet Gimel Dalet
Peh Kaf Bet Gimel Dalet

Bet Dalet Gimel Kaf Peh
Bet Dalet Gimel Peh Kaf
Bet Dalet Peh Gimel Kaf
Bet Peh Dalet Gimel Kaf
Peh Bet Dalet Gimel Kaf

Bet Dalet Kaf Gimel Peh
Bet Dalet Kaf Peh Gimel
Bet Dalet Peh Kaf Gimel
Bet Peh Dalet Kaf Gimel
Peh Bet Dalet Kaf Gimel

Bet Kaf Dalet Gimel Peh
Bet Kaf Dalet Peh Gimel
Bet Kaf Peh Dalet Gimel
Bet Peh Kaf Dalet Gimel
Peh Bet Kaf Dalet Gimel

Kaf Bet Dalet Gimel Peh
Kaf Bet Dalet Peh Gimel
Kaf Bet Peh Dalet Gimel
Kaf Peh Bet Dalet Gimel
Peh Kaf Bet Dalet Gimel

Gimel Bet Dalet Kaf Peh
Gimel Bet Dalet Peh Kaf
Gimel Bet Peh Dalet Kaf
Gimel Peh Bet Dalet Kaf
Peh Gimel Bet Dalet Kaf

Gimel Bet Kaf Dalet Peh
Gimel Bet Kaf Peh Dalet
Gimel Bet Peh Kaf Dalet
Gimel Peh Bet Kaf Dalet
Peh Gimel Bet Kaf Dalet

Gimel Kaf Bet Dalet Peh
Gimel Kaf Bet Peh Dalet
Gimel Kaf Peh Bet Dalet
Gimel Peh Kaf Bet Dalet
Peh Gimel Kaf Bet Dalet

Kaf Gimel Bet Dalet Peh
Kaf Gimel Bet Peh Dalet
Kaf Gimel Peh Bet Dalet
Kaf Peh Gimel Bet Dalet
Peh Kaf Gimel Bet Dalet

Gimel Dalet Bet Kaf Peh
Gimel Dalet Bet Peh Kaf
Gimel Dalet Peh Bet Kaf
Gimel Peh Dalet Bet Kaf
Peh Gimel Dalet Bet Kaf

Gimel Dalet Kaf Bet Peh
Gimel Dalet Kaf Peh Bet
Gimel Dalet Peh Kaf Bet
Gimel Peh Dalet Kaf Bet
Peh Gimel Dalet Kaf Bet

Gimel Kaf Dalet Bet Peh
Gimel Kaf Dalet Peh Bet
Gimel Kaf Peh Dalet Bet
Gimel Peh Kaf Dalet Bet
Peh Gimel Kaf Dalet Bet

Kaf Gimel Dalet Bet Peh
Kaf Gimel Dalet Peh Bet
Kaf Gimel Peh Dalet Bet
Kaf Peh Gimel Dalet Bet
Peh Kaf Gimel Dalet Bet

Dalet Bet Gimel Kaf Peh
Dalet Bet Gimel Peh Kaf
Dalet Bet Peh Gimel Kaf
Dalet Peh Bet Gimel Kaf
Peh Dalet Bet Gimel Kaf

Dalet Bet Kaf Gimel Peh
Dalet Bet Kaf Peh Gimel
Dalet Bet Peh Kaf Gimel
Dalet Peh Bet Kaf Gimel
Peh Dalet Bet Kaf Gimel

Dalet Kaf Bet Gimel Peh
Dalet Kaf Bet Peh Gimel
Dalet Kaf Peh Bet Gimel
Dalet Peh Kaf Bet Gimel
Peh Dalet Kaf Bet Gimel

Kaf Dalet Bet Gimel Peh
Kaf Dalet Bet Peh Gimel
Kaf Dalet Peh Bet Gimel
Kaf Peh Dalet Bet Gimel
Peh Kaf Dalet Bet Gimel

Dalet Gimel Bet Kaf Peh
Dalet Gimel Bet Peh Kaf
Dalet Gimel Peh Bet Kaf
Dalet Peh Gimel Bet Kaf
Peh Dalet Gimel Bet Kaf

Dalet Gimel Kaf Bet Peh
Dalet Gimel Kaf Peh Bet
Dalet Gimel Peh Kaf Bet
Dalet Peh Gimel Kaf Bet
Peh Dalet Gimel Kaf Bet

Dalet Kaf Gimel Bet Peh
Dalet Kaf Gimel Peh Bet
Dalet Kaf Peh Gimel Bet
Dalet Peh Kaf Gimel Bet
Peh Dalet Kaf Gimel Bet

Kaf Dalet Gimel Bet Peh
Kaf Dalet Gimel Peh Bet
Kaf Dalet Peh Gimel Bet
Kaf Peh Dalet Gimel Bet
Peh Kaf Dalet Gimel Bet

Chapter Five
The Law of Twelve: *Heh, Vav, Zayin, Chet, Tet, Yod, Lamed, Nun, Samech, Ayin, Tzadi, Kuf*

Chapter Five lists the twelve single letters and describes what their creative powers bring into the Universe, Year and Humanity. The single letters, unlike the double letters, have only one pronunciation.

Verse 5:1 Twelve Single Letters

The twelve single letters—Heh, Vav, Zayin, Chet*, Tet, Yod, Lamed, Nun, Samech, Ayin, Tzadi, Kuf—are speaking, thinking, walking, seeing, hearing, walking, intercourse, smelling, sleeping, anger, tasting and laughter.

The seven double letters created qualities of being: life, peace, wisdom, wealth, beauty, fruitfulness, and power). The twelve single letters create *activities*: seeing, hearing, smelling, speaking, eating, intercourse, action, walking, anger, laughter, thought, and sleep. Activities may be present or absent, but they have no opposites; thus, they are symbolized by the twelve single letters. Of these twelve activities, three are sensory activities (hearing, seeing, smelling); three are bodily needs (eating, sleeping, intercourse); three are physical abilities (working, walking, speaking); and three are mind/heart activities (thought, anger and laughter). Just as every individual does

---

*Note that "Ch" is a guttural sound in the back of the throat

---

not possess all seven qualities in equal measure, each individual does not possess equal ability to engage in the twelve activities. Some of us cannot see, some cannot walk, etc., but these are important aspects of the *overall* human experience.

The twelve single letters correspond to the twelve diagonal paths on the Tree of Life; see Figure 15, **Twelve Single Letters on the Tree**. Working with these letters in various ways (contemplation, chanting, writing, etc.) allows us to move up and down on the Tree.

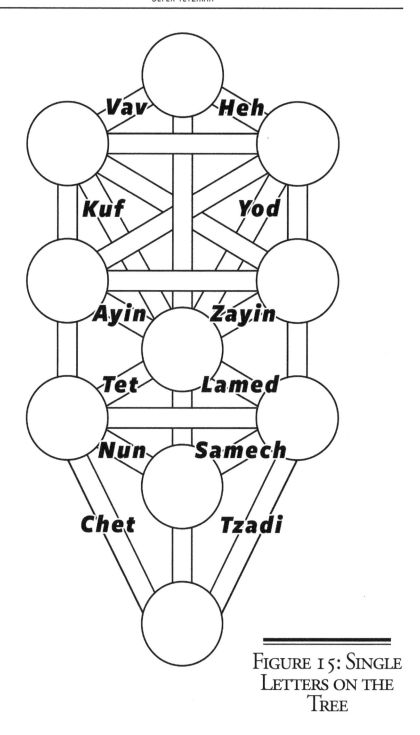

FIGURE 15: SINGLE
LETTERS ON THE
TREE

Suggestions for working with Verse 5:1 ═══════

1. Consider the twelve activities listed here. What is your relationship with them? Are any of them more a focus in your life than others? Do any of them pose a particular difficulty for you, either because you do too much of it or too little?

2. To what extent do these activities sum up human life? Are there important activities that aren't included in these twelve?

Verse 5:2 Twelve Boundaries of Space

Twelve single letters: they form twelve diagonal boundaries: northeast, southeast, east above, east below, north above, north below, southwest, northwest, west above, west below, south above, south below. They widen and continue into eternity of eternities; they are the arms of the universe.

The single letters correspond to the 12 diagonal boundaries of a cube. Most translators do not attempt to assign particular letters to particular boundaries, though Kaplan provides the assignment of letters and directions given by Rabbi Elijah ben Shlomo Zalman (1720–1797). Contemplating these letters and their associated directions can send the mind out to the boundaries of the universe. These letters and directions may also be used to mentally create a cube. See Figure 16, **Twelve Single Letters on a Cube**.[47]

With respect to exercises such as these, Kaplan makes this statement. "A very important element in attaining the mystical experience is the negation of the self. When a person sees himself as nothing, then his self becomes transparent to the Divine. Commenting on the phrase, 'from under the arms of the universe,' the Talmud states that a person must 'make himself like he does not exist.' Through contemplating the infinities of the universe, one can nullify the ego."[48] Nullification of the ego is not a goal of mainstream Jewish practice; however, the *Sefer Yetzirah* is a mystical texts. As with mystical texts from other traditions, it is an expression of the Oneness of the Universe. The initiated know that the ego is a by-product of culture and history and has no independent existence.

The phrase "eternity of eternities" means beyond space and time; this is God's true home. The phrase "the arms of the universe" comes from Deuteronomy 33:26–27, and refers to the dimensions of physical space: "There is none like the God of Jeshuran; the rider of the heavens is your Helper; His pride is in the skies. A dwelling is the God of eternity and

---

47 Kaplan, Aryeh. *Sefer Yetzirah: The Book of Creation.* York Beach, ME: Samuel Weiser, Inc., 1997, p. 204.

48 Kaplan, Aryeh. *Sefer Yetzirah: The Book of Creation.* York Beach, ME: Samuel Weiser, Inc., 1997, p. 204.

below are the arms of the universe." The analogy used in Jewish mysticism for God becoming visible in space and time is God riding in His Chariot; thus, the reference here to "the rider of the heavens." It is only when God rides forth into space and time that prophets such as Ezekiel can perceive Him.

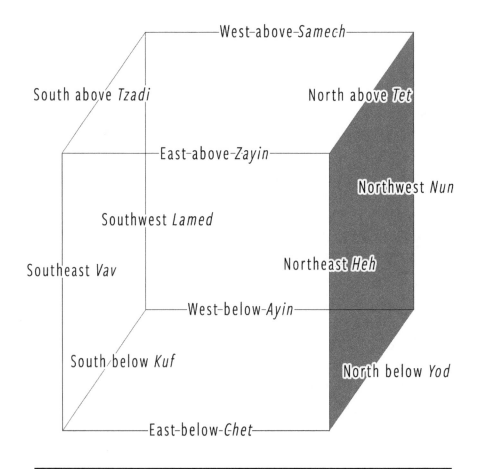

FIGURE 16: TWELVE SINGLE LETTERS ON A CUBE

Suggestions for working with Verse 5:2

1. Create the Cube of Space around you. Begin by facing north. Start by creating the three dimensions of width, depth and height. Start with your own dimensions to make this manageable. Chant *Mem* to create the dimension of width, your own width, the width of your hips or your shoulders. Chant *Shin* to create the dimension of depth, from your front to your back. Chant *Alef* to create the dimension of height, from your feet to your head. Lock these three dimensions in place by chanting *Mem Shin Alef*. Hold these three dimensions in your head for a minute.

Now construct a square around your feet. Look down at the ground in front of your feet and visualize a line right in front of you; chant *Yod*. Now visualize a line behind your feet and chant *Kuf*. On your right-hand side, visualize a new line connecting the *Yod* line in front of you with the *Kuf* line behind you; chant *Chet*. On your left-hand side, visualize a new line connecting the *Yod* line in front of you with the *Kuf* line behind you; chant *Ayin*. Now let's lock that square into place by chanting *Yod, Kuf, Chet, Ayin*.

Now construct a square above your head. Look above your head and in front of you and visualize a line there; chant *Tet*. Now visualize a line behind your head and chant *Tzadi*. On the right-hand side above you, visualize a new line connecting the *Tet* line in front of you with the *Tzadi* line behind you; chant *Zayin*. On the left-hand side above you, visualize a new line connecting the *Tet* line in front of you with the *Tzadi* line behind you; chant *Samech*. Now let's lock that square into place by chanting *Tet, Tzadi, Zayin, Samech*.

Now construct four pillars connecting the square above with the square below. Reach your right hand out in front of you and feel the pillar that connects the square above with the square below in front of you and to the right; chant *Heh*. Reach your right hand out behind you and feel the pillar that connects the square above with the square below behind you and to the right; chant *Vav*. Reach your left hand out in front of you and feel the pillar that connects the square above with the square below in front of you and to the left; chant *Nun*. Reach your left hand out behind you and feel the pillar that connects the square above with the square below behind you and to the left; chant *Lamed*.

Finally, find the center of your being. Touch it with your awareness and chant *Tav*. This is the spark of the One God that lives within you. This is a personal-sized cube, which you can create any time you feel the need for safety or centering.

Verse 5:3 The Twelve in the Universe, Year and Humanity

*The twelve single letters—Heh, Vav, Zayin, Chet, Tet, Yod, Lamed,
Nun, Samech, Ayin, Tzadi, Kuf—He engraved them, hewed them,
weighed them, interchanged them, combined them, and formed with
them the twelve constellations in the Universe, twelve months in the
Year and twelve organs in Humanity, male and female.*

The same process used for the three mothers and seven doubles are used
now for the seven simple letters. They are engraved, hewed, weighed,
interchanged, combined and formed, so that they form aspects of the five
dimensions of creation: height, width, depth, time and spirituality.

The 12 single letters also reflect the 12 permutations of God's name:
YVHH, YHHV, HVHY, HVYH, HHVY, HVHY, VHYH, VHHY, VYHH,
HYHV, HYVH, HHYV, YHVH. See Figure 17, **Twelve Permutations of
the Tetragrammaton on a Cube.**

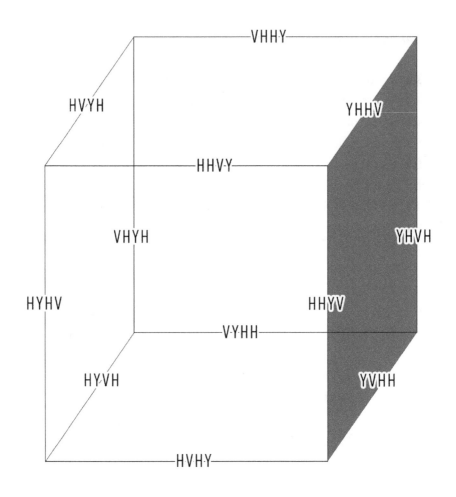

FIGURE 17: TWELVE PERMUTATIONS OF THE
TETRAGRAMMATON ON A CUBE

Suggestions for working with Verse 5:3

1. Visualize yourself standing in the center of the cube pictured in Figure 17, **Twelve Permutations of the Tetragrammaton on a Cube**. Draw a square around your head by chanting *Vav Heh Heh Yod*, *Yod Heh Heh Vav*, *Heh Vav Yod Heh* and *Heh Heh Vav Yod*. Draw a square at your feet by chanting *Vav Yod Heh Heh*, *Heh Yod Vav Heh*, *Heh Vav Heh Yod* and *Yod Vav Heh Heh*. Connect the squares by chanting *Heh Yod Heh Vav*, *Vav Heh Yod Heh*, *Heh Heh Yod Vav* and *Yod Heh Vav Heh*. You are surrounded by the name of God.

2. Visualize yourself as surrounded by a protective sphere; chant the twelve permutations of the Tetragrammaton and watch the sphere become increasingly powerful which each permutation: *Vav Heh Heh Yod*, *Yod Heh Heh Vav*, *Heh Vav Yod Heh*, *Heh Heh Vav Yod*, *Vav Yod Heh Heh*, *Heh Yod Vav Heh*, *Heh Vav Heh Yod*, *Yod Vav Heh Heh*, *Heh Yod Heh Vav*, *Vav Heh Yod Heh*, *Heh Heh Yod Vav*, *Yod Heh Vav Heh*.

Verse 5:4 The Twelve Single Letters in the Universe: Constellations

The twelve constellations in the Universe are Aries (T'leh), Taurus (Shor), Gemini (Teumim), Cancer (Sartan), Leo (Ari), Virgo (Betulah), Libra (Maznayim), Scorpio (Akrav), Sagittarius (Keshet), Capricorn (Gedi), Aquarius (Deli), Pisces (Dagin).

The constellation names in common use today are from ancient Greece; however, astrological systems were in place as early as the 2nd millennium B.C.E. in Babylonia.

The Hebrew constellation names are simply Hebrew versions of the Greek constellation names; *Ari* means "lion", *Gedi* means "goat", etc. In this case, the constellations are viewed as physical entities. There is no suggestion that the *Sefer Yetzirah* is a proponent of astrology.

However, ancient Jewish practices did engage in astrology. As Gershom Scholem explains, "At the same time, practical Kabbalah did manifest an interest in the magical induction of the pneumatic powers of the stars through the agency of specific charms. ... Interestingly, Kabbalistic attitudes toward astrological magic were highly ambivalent, and some leading Kabbalists, such as Cordovero, actually approved of it."[49]

Correspondences between the letters and the constellations are as follows: Aries is assigned to *Heh*, Taurus to *Vav*, Gemini to *Zayin*, Cancer to *Chet*, Leo to *Tet*, Virgo to *Yod*, Libra to *Lamed*, Scorpio to *Nun*, Sagittarius to *Samech*, Capricorn to *Ayin*, Aquarius to *Tzadi*, and Pisces to *Kuf*

Suggestions for working with Verse 5:4

1. Select the Hebrew letter that corresponds with your birth sign. Chant that letter and visualize your birth sign's constellation being formed by that letter.

---

49 Scholem, Gershom. *Kabbalah.* New York, NY: Dorset Press, 1974, pp. 186-189.

Verse 5:5 Twelve Single Letters in the Year: Months

The twelve months in the Universe are Nissan, Iyar, Sivan, Tamuz, Av, Elul, Tishrei, Marcheshvan, Kislev, Tevet, Shevat, Adar.

There are twelve months in both the Hebrew and Roman calendars, though the Hebrew calendar includes a leap month (called *Adar 2*) seven times every nineteen years. The names of the twelve Hebrew months, shown in the Verse above, are Babylonian in origin; in the Torah, the months are usually referred to as "the first month," "the second month," and so on. There are months mentioned that are not used today: the month of *Aviv* is mentioned in Exodus 13:4, *Ziv* is mentioned in 1 Kings 6:1, 37; *Ethanim* is mentioned in 1 Kings 8:2; and *Bul* is mentioned in 1 Kings 6:38.

Nissan is March/April; Iyar is April/May; Sivan is May/June; Tamuz is June/July; Av is July/August; Elul is August/September; Tishrei is September/October; Marcheshvan is October/November; Kislev is November/December; Tevet is December/January; Shevat is January/February and Adar is February/March.

Other time-related "twelves" are the twelve hours in the day and the twelve hours in the night.

Suggestions for working with Verse 5:5

1. Consider the cycle of time. Spend some quiet time contemplating the cycles of your own life: the ups and downs of your career, your relationships, your understanding of yourself. What part of the cycle are you in right now?

2. What "twelves" exist in your world? Watch for the appearance of the number twelve this week.

Verse 5:6 The Twelve Single Letters in Humanity

Twelve parts of the Person: two hands, two feet, two kidneys, gall bladder, hemsess, liver, korkeban, kivah, spleen.

There are three unfamiliar body parts referenced in this Verse: *hemsess*, *korkeban* and *kivah*. *Hemsess* means the third stomach in ruminating animals, but is generally believed to correspond to the small intestine. *Korkeban* is sometimes translated as "gizzard", though stomach appears to be the most popular choice. *Kivah* is the fouth stomach in ruminants; our ancestors were far more familiar with the anatomy of cows and birds (which were butchered for food) than the anatomy of humans (which were, presumably, not butchered for food).

Typically, translators replace these three mysterious words with a selection of the following: esophagus, small intestine, large intestine, colon, bowels, gall, stomach, and even (a minority opinion from Westcott in the Victorian Age) "private parts." Modern students may use stomach, colon and intestines for the exercises in this chapter.

Suggestions for working with Verse 5:6

1. Lie on your back. In your mind's eye, envision the Hebrew letters creating the organs within your body. Don't be concerned at this point about which letter created which organ; simply watch the letters at work. See them glowing with health and vitality as they create this wonderful physical body for your use.

2. Consider the possibility that *hemsess*, *korkeban* and *kivah* are three mystery organs that are responsible for creating intuition, the ability to interpret dreams and the mystic connection to God. In your mind's eye, envision the Hebrew letters creating these three mysterious and invisible organs, which were known to our ancestors but not to modern science, within your body.

Verse 5:7 Heh, Vav and Zayin

He made the letter Heh king over speaking. He bound a crown to it, combined one with another and formed Aries in the Universe, Nissan in the Year and the right hand in Humanity, male and female.

He made the letter Vav king over thinking. He bound a crown to it, combined one with another and formed Taurus in the Universe, Iyar in the Year and the left hand in Humanity, male and female.

He made the letter Zayin king over laughing. He bound a crown to it, combined one with another and formed Gemini in the Universe, Sivan in the Year and the liver in Humanity, male and female.

Verse 5:8 Chet, Tet and Yod

He made the letter Chet king over anger. He bound a crown to it, combined one with another and formed Cancer in the Universe, Tamuz in the Year and the pancreas in Humanity, male and female.

He made the letter Tet king over seeing. He bound a crown to it, combined one with another and formed Leo in the Universe, Av in the Year and the gall bladder in Humanity, male and female.

He made the letter Yod king over hearing. He bound a crown to it, combined one with another and formed Virgo in the Universe, Elul in the Year and the spleen in Humanity, male and female.

Verse 5:9 Lamed, Nun and Samech

He made the letter Lamed king over smelling. He bound a crown to it, combined one with another and formed Libra in the Universe, Tishrei in the Year and the right kidney in Humanity, male and female.

He made the letter Nun king over tasting. He bound a crown to it, combined one with another and formed Scorpio in the Universe, Marcheshvan in the Year and the large intestine in Humanity, male and female.

He made the letter Samekh king over intercourse. He bound a crown to it, combined one with another and formed Sagittarius in the Universe, Kislev in the Year and the intestines in Humanity, male and female.

Verse 5:10 Ayin, Tzadi and Kuf

He made the letter Ayin king over sleeping. He bound a crown to it, combined one with another and formed Capricorn in the Universe, Tivet in the Year and the colon in Humanity, male and female.

He made the letter Tzdi king over walking. He bound a crown to it, combined one with another and formed Aquarius in the Universe, Shevat in the Year and the right foot in Humanity, male and female.

He made the letter Kuf king over working. He bound a crown to it, combined one with another and formed Pisces in the Universe, Adar in the Year and the left foot in Humanity, male and female.

He made them like a war, arranged them like a wall, set one against the other in battle.

The remaining Verses of this chapter assign an activity, constellation, month and body part to each of the single letters. Translators generally just take the activities as they are listed in their version of the *Sefer Yetzirah* and assign them in that order to the letters.

Some correspondences between activities and body parts are based on an old belief that certain body parts affect human behavior: "Two discontented or insulting: the liver, the gall. Two jolly or laughing: the colon, the spleen. Two advising: the kidneys. Two taking advice: the stomach, the bowels (rectum). Two robbing: the hands. Two hunting: the feet."[50] Glotzer quotes the Rokeach (Rabbi Eliezer of Garmiza): "The falsifiers are the gall bladder and the kidneys, which excite a person and cause him

---

50 Kalisch, Rev. Dr. Isidor and Stenring, Knut. *Sepher Yetzirah: The Book of Creation.* San Diego, CA: The Book Tree, 2006, p. 108.

falseness. The two happy ones are the stomach and the spleen, which gladden people—the stomach with eating and drinking and the spleen with laughter. The two advisors are the two kidneys, as it is said, 'I will bless God who advised me, even at night my kidneys admonished me' (Psalms 16:7)."[51]

Glotzer gives an example of another way in which these matches are made by explaining the rationale used by Raivad (R. Avraham ben David, father of Isaac the Blind) to assign *Vav* to the left hand. " 'He made *Vav* king—Taurus, the face of the ox, is through the strength of the *Vav* of the letters *Hey*, *Vav*, *Zayin*, *Chet*, *Tet*, *Yod*, *Lamed*, *Nun*, *Samech*, *Ayin*, *Tzadi*, and *Kuf*. It is associated with the left hand for 'The face of the ox is to the left of the four of them' (Ezekiel 1:10).' "[52]

Given that there is no hard and fast rule on how these correspondences are designed, the modern student is certainly free to create his own associations. The *Sefer Yetzirah: Magic and Mysticism* uses correspondences derived from group work and contemplation. See Table 5 for a summary of single letters and their correspondences.

As with all the assignments and correspondences, the student is free to accept those in common use or to create his own. There are advantages and disadvantages either way. It is generally accepted that group energy adds a great deal of power; the more often a correspondence has been used, the more power or energy surrounds it. As a result, most students find it easier to use commonly accepted correspondences. The correspondences of the mother letters, for example, are so well-known and widely-accepted that changing *Aleph* to water and *Mem* to air would be an uphill battle for the student's contemplation practice.

However, less widely known correspondences may be altered with some ease. In the case of the double and single letters, because there has

---

51 Glotzer, Leonard R. *The Fundamentals of Jewish Mysticism: The Book of Creation and Its Commentaries.* Northvale, NJ: Jason Aronson, Inc., 1992, p. 178.

52 Glotzer, Leonard R. *The Fundamentals of Jewish Mysticism: The Book of Creation and Its Commentaries.* Northvale, NJ: Jason Aronson, Inc., 1992, p. 181.

been no agreement among rabbis, scholars and occultists, we are sometimes best served by creating our own assignments and correspondences. When working with a school or group, of course, the student should follow the tradition of that group, but the solitary student is free to follow his own inclination. As Bill Whitcomb explain, "Few published systems (or the rituals constructed using them) are as meaningful to the reader as to the author. Many religious and magical traditions are chiefly the commemoration of someone else's attainments. At their worst, older systems are little more than the leftover roadmaps of various travelers."[53]

This last sentence of Verse 5:10 is an important one. Glotzer quotes the *Otzar HaShem*, a commentary on the *Mishnah*: "[*Sefer Yetzirah*] says that the Infinite made the world, the year, and the soul like a war. What is meant is that each of the twelve leaders in the world, year, and soul appear to be in conflict with each other. Aries, Leo, and Capricorn are fire. Taurus, Virgo, and Sagittarius are air. Gemini, Libra, and Aquarius are wind. Cancer, Scorpio, and Pisces are water. Those of water fight with those of fire. Those of air fight with those of wind. Some acquit and some convict. Some kill and some make live. Some are hot and wet and some cold and dry . . . So is it with the [leaders of the] soul. Some are active, some are passive. So is it in the year—He made four opposite seasons. After the heat He always puts the moderate temperature. After the summer, which is hot and dry, He brought the fall, which is cold and wet. Likewise, the spring, which is warm and wet, comes after the winter, which is cold and dry. He did so in order to avoid going from extreme to extreme and causing great change and thus bad happenings. Therefore, in His great wisdom, He made them like a fight and stationed them like in a war. *Sefer Yetzirah* says "like" a war, for these things are not [conflicts] with words or with physical swords but rather result from the combinations and their reflections one on the other."[54]

53 Whitcomb, Bill. *The Magician's Companion*. Woodbury, MN: Llewellyn Publications, 2007, pp. 24-25.

54 Glotzer, Leonard R. *The Fundamentals of Jewish Mysticism: The Book of Creation and Its Commentaries*. Northvale, NJ: Jason Aronson, Inc., 1992, p. 179.

We see that the elements of nature are viewed as being in opposition to one another, and it is this opposition that allows the natural world to function. The "wall" refers to the zodiacal circle. Similarly, there are attributes of man that are in opposition to one another. Since 12 has no center point, no place of balance; there is no place of balance between the attributes discussed in this Chapter. The warring of the twelve cannot be resolved on this level; it can only be resolved by going "up" from the level of "action" to the higher level of "being." The level of being (the Sevens) has a center; the level of actions (the Twelves) does not.

Suggestions for working with Verses 5:7 through 5:10

1. Consider the four sensory activities created by the single letters: seeing, hearing, smelling and tasting. Chanting the letters responsible for these activities can help us to give them added power. When you are next in a situation requiring better sight, try chanting *Tet* to improve your sight. Similarly, chanting *Yod* might help us to hear better. Chanting can also help on a metaphysical level; if we need to "see" or "hear" the truth of a situation, chanting the appropriate letter may give our seeing or hearing abilities the boost they need.

2. Contemplate the activities of speaking, thinking and working. These are all different ways in which we create our world, though we typically use them unconsciously. Consider the roles of speech, thought and work in the creation of your own world. What might you do to use these abilities to create a world more to your liking?

3. Anger is included in the twelve activities, ranked equally with such essentials as sleeping and eating. Contemplate the role of anger in your life. Are you afraid of anger, either your own or that of others? What would a healthy relationship with anger look and feel like? Since anger comes into being through a single letter rather than a double letter, the

Sefer Yetzirah does not believe that anger has an opposite. Do you agree with that?

4. Using Table 6, **Single Letter Correspondences**, note the letters which correspond to areas of your body that you may feel need some special attention. Creating a chant from these letters can help direct healing energy to the right areas. For example, someone with a family history of liver disease who is prone to earaches in the right ear might chant *Kaf Zayin* several times a day.

TABLE 6: SINGLE LETTER CORRESPONDENCES

Letter	Activity	Direction	Constellation	Months	Body Part	Path
Heh	Speaking	Northeast	Aries	*Nissan*	Right hand	Keter-Chokmah
Vav	Thinking	Southeast	Taurus	*Iyar*	Left hand	Keter-Binah
Zayin	Laughing	East above	Gemini	*Sivan*	Liver	Chokmah-Tifaret
Chet	Anger	East below	Cancer	*Tamuz*	Pancreas	Binah-Tifaret
Tet	Seeing	North above	Leo	*Av*	Gall bladder	Chesed-Tifaret
Yod	Hearing	North below	Virgo	*Elul*	Spleen	Gevurah-Tifaret
Lamed	Smelling	Southwest	Libra	*Tishrei*	Right kidney	Tifaret-Netzach
Nun	Tasting	Northwest	Scorpio	*Marcheshvan*	Left kidney	Tifaret-Hod
Samech	Intercours	West above	Sagittarius	*Kislev*	Intestines	Netzach-Yesod
Ayin	Sleeping	West below	Capricorn	*Tivet*	Colon	Gevurah-Yesdo
Tzadi	Walking	South above	Aquarius	*Shevat*	Right foot	Netzach-Malkuth
Kuf	Working	South below	Pisces	*Adar*	Left foot	Hod-Malkuth

Chapter Six
The Three Laws

This Chapter restates Verse 3:2, explaining that the three physical elements of air, water and fire are called the Three Fathers; they emanated from the three mother letters, *Alef*, *Mem* and *Shin*. In turn, the Three Fathers created the seven planets and twelve diagonal boundaries in physical space.

Verse 6:1 True Witnesses

These are the Three Mothers: Aleph Mem Shin. From them emanated Three Fathers, and they are air, water, and fire. From the three Fathers descended seven planets and their hosts, and twelve diagonal boundaries. Proving this are true witnesses in the Universe, Year, Humanity. He decreed twelve, seven, and three, and assigned them to Teli, Cycle, and Heart.

What are the true witnesses and to what do they testify? The witnesses are the patterns of three, seven and twelve found in physical space, in time, and in humanity. The underlying patterns of the cosmos testify to the existence of a Creator. Glotzer quotes Raivad (R. Avraham ben David, father of Isaac the Blind): "Proving the matter are the reliable witnesses of world, year, and soul. For all that is in the soul can be found in the year and the world, and similarly with each of the others. These are reliable witnesses that they are all derived from one source."[55]

The idea that the similarity of construction in physical space, time and mankind, shown by the patterns of three, seven and twelve, proves that physical space, time and mankind all came from One Designer is the fundamental argument of the *Sefer Yetzirah*. This argument may not seem terribly convincing; however, most people base their personal belief in God on the patterns of their own lives—unsought miracles, unexpected synchronicities, and so on. The human need for and ability to perceive patterns causes us to experience God *in* patterns and *as* patterns.

The last sentence tells us that God put the patterns of three, seven and twelve into the Teli, the Cycle and the Heart. In previous chapters, the dimensions are described as Universe, Time and Humanity; this is the first time the Teli, Cycle and Heart are mentioned. However, as we shall see, this new choice of words is quite deliberate.

The *Teli* is a rather mysterious word found in neither the Bible nor the Talmud. It is generally felt to be an imaginary axis about which the heavens rotate; the *Teli* is the center point of the world. The *Teli* has also been described as a dragon, whose power moves the zodiac.

The word used for Cycle is *Galgal*; it denotes the unfolding of time or the cycle of events in the world. This same word is used in Verse 2:4, meaning "circle": the 22 letters are fixed in a *Galgal* with 231 gates. The Cycle is the central concept of the dimension of time.

"Heart" is used in this Verse because it is the center of the body. It seems odd that the heart is referenced here, as it is not one of the body parts mentioned in the earlier chapters, but it is clear that "heart" is intended to mean the center of the human body.

Taken as a whole, the *Teli*, Cycle and Heart are intended to relate, respectively, to Universe, Year and Person; *Teli* is the prime mover or central point of the Universe; the Cycle is the prime mover or central point of the

---

55 Glotzer, Leonard R. *The Fundamentals of Jewish Mysticism: The Book of Creation and Its Commentaries.* Northvale, NJ: Jason Aronson, Inc., 1992, p. 192.

Year; the Heart is the prime mover or central point of the Person. As Meyer Waxman, author of the six-volume *A History of Jewish Literature*, explains: "Our author is, however, anxious to show the unity in this manifold and he states that each system is dominated by a center. The center of the external world is the Teli, which is the axis of the world, sometimes called the line of the *Drakon* (dragon), the center of the year is the revolution of the sphere of constellations, and that of man, the heart."[56]

Suggestions for working with this Verse:

1. Are you aware of patterns in the universe? Do you feel these patterns reveal the hand of the creator? Or are you more inclined to see God in the apparent exceptions to the patterns, i.e., miracles?

2. What patterns do you see in your own life? What conclusions about yourself or God have you drawn from these patterns?

56 Waxman, Meyer. *A History of Jewish Literature: Volume 1.* NY, NY: Thomas Yoseloff, 1960, p. 392.

Verse 6:2 Fire, Water and Air

The three are fire, water, and air. Fire is above, water is below, and air mediates between them. This is symbolized by "fire carrying water." Mem hums, Shin hisses, and Aleph is the breath of air that mediates between them.

The statement that fire is above, water is below, and air mediates between them refers to fire as symbolic of heaven, water as symbolic of seas and earth, and air as symbolic of the atmosphere that separates them. Similarly, fire symbolizes spirit, water symbolizes the body (recall that the element of earth is believed to emanate from water, as shown in Verse 3.4), and air symbolizes the mind. How does the mind mediate between body and soul? The body is representative of the "animal" part of our nature and spirit is representative of the "angel" part of our nature; the mind bridges the gap by making us aware of and able to mediate between, the animal and angel aspects.

But how does fire carry water? This means that spirit is actually the foundation of the body. Our body does not carry us; it is our spirit that moves or "carries" us.

The Verse concludes by pointing out that the corresponding element of each letter is seen in the sound of the letter itself. Thus, *Mem* hums like the sound of moving water, *Shin* hisses like fire, and *Aleph* is silent like air.

Suggestions for working with this Verse:

1. Do you experience yourself as a body (water) carrying a soul (fire)? Or as a soul carrying a body? Envision these different views and experience the change in perspective. Does one feel truer than the other? Or do both feel true?

Verse 6:3 Teli, Cycle and Heart

The Teli in the Universe is like a king on his throne. The Cycle in the Year is like a king in his kingdom. The Heart in the Person is like a king in war.

God, symbolized by a king, is at the center of all the dimensions. The phrase "King on his throne" refers to God in *Malkuth*, i.e., in the physical world. The throne is the symbol of the king's power and stability; it also separates the king from the kingdom. Similarly, the *Teli* is separate from the cosmos; it is the axis that remains motionless while the cosmos moves. The *Teli*, then, is the throne of God in physical space.

The Cycle refers to the dimension of time. While the *Teli* is separate from the cosmos and the throne separates the king from the kingdom, the Cycle is not separate from time. The Cycle is an intrinsic part of the dimension of time. Similarly, when the king is in his kingdom, he is part of the kingdom.

Finally, "the king in war" symbolizes conflict. The "Person" in the Verse is the dimension of mankind and spirituality. It is here that opposites come into being. Neither physical space nor time can contain opposites. And it is the emergence of opposites that creates conflict.

Another view of this Verse is that when we rest comfortably in the physical world, unaware of time and the conflict of opposites, we are present and at peace. When we become aware of the dimension of time, we begin to think about past and future. At this point, we have left the security of the throne and are out "in the kingdom". When we add in the various personal difficulties that arise from opposites (good and evil, wealth and poverty, beauty and ugliness, etc.), we find ourselves embroiled in conflict.

Suggestions for working with this Verse:

1. Consider what it means in your own life to be on your throne, in your kingdom and at war. Are these physical places? Or states of mind?

Verse 6:4 Good and Evil

God set one opposite the other: good opposite evil, evil opposite good. Good comes from good and evil from evil; good defines evil and evil defines good. Good is kept for the good ones and evil is kept for the evil ones.

This Verse speaks about the spiritual dimension, in which good and evil are opposing forces. Good and evil exist in equal measure: there is not more good than evil or more evil than good. Everything in the Universe is in perfect balance.

All opposites define one another. Cold is the absence of heat; darkness is the absence of light. Thus, if evil did not exist, we would not have something defined as good and vice versa. Several translators use the word "tests" in place of "defines". The idea of evil testing the good implies that evil things come to good people as a test: will they turn away from their goodness as a result of this evil? Similarly, good things come to evil people as a test: will they turn away from their evil as a result of this good?

Eventually, "Good is kept for the good ones and evil is kept for the evil ones", perhaps implying that in the next world good people are rewarded by good, and evil people are rewarded by evil in an after-life or by karma. This should not lead us to expect an after-life filled with physical or sensual delights; the ultimate reward is nearness to God.

Suggestions for working with this Verse:

1. What is your relationship to good and evil? Do you recognize the balance of good and evil in the world? Do you feel that there is more good than evil or more evil than good?

Verse 6:5 Positive, Negative and Neutral

Three, each one stands alone. One is positive, one is negative, one is neutral and balances the other two. Seven, three are divided against three, with one balancing the others. Twelve are at war: three that love, three that hate, three that give life and three that give death. The three that love are the heart and ears; the three that hate are the liver, gall bladder and tongue; the three that give life are the two nostrils and the spleen; the three that give death are the two lower openings and the mouth. God, faithful King, rules over them all, One above three; three above seven, seven above twelve, all linked together.

As we have seen throughout the *Sefer Yetzirah*, the underlying pattern of the universe is thesis, antithesis and resolution; or positive, negative and neutral. In the division of three, one acts as thesis, one acts as antithesis, and one acts as resolution. In the division of seven, three act as thesis, three act as antithesis, and one acts as resolution. But it isn't possible to divide twelve into an equal number of thesis and antithesis with one left to resolve. This is why the twelve are always associated with war: there is no resolution. However, the One, the principle of resolution, manifests in the division of twelve as the principle of individuality.

"*One above three; three above seven, seven above twelve, all linked together.*" The point here is that from the One come the Law of Three, the Law of Seven, and the Law of Twelve, expressed through the five dimensions of space, time and spirituality.

The twelve organs referenced here as being "at war" are the heart, ears, liver, gall bladder, tongue, two nostrils, spleen, mouth and the two excretory openings. The liver, gall bladder and spleen are included in the list of the twelve organs given in Chapter Five; the ears, nostrils and mouth are included in the list of seven openings given in Chapter Four. The heart is in the chest, one of the three body parts given in Chapter Three. The tongue and excretory openings are not in any of the earlier lists.

This new list of twelve is arranged in four groups of three each. The general consensus is that the heart and ears are the lovers; the liver, gall bladder and tongue are the haters; the two nostrils and the spleen are the life-givers; the two excretory openings and the mouth are the death-givers. We see that the list is arranged as pairs of opposites: lovers and haters, life-givers and death-givers.

Suggestions for working with this Verse:

1. How do you feel about this idea of your body being at war? Are there aspects of your body that seem to be at peace and others that are at war?

Verse 6:6 All That Ever Was

These are the twenty-two letters with which engraved Ehyeh, Yah, YHVH Elohim, YHVH, YHVH Tzavaot, Elohim Tzavaot, El Shaddai, YHVH Adonoy. He created three Books and with them created His whole Universe, forming with them all that was ever formed, and all that ever will be formed.

This Verse recalls Verse 1:1 by giving us many names of God and referencing the three Books (number, letter and expression) used to create the Universe. The three Books may also reference the three divisions of letters: Mothers, Doubles and Singles. The Verse explains that everything that was created, as well as everything that was to be created in the future, came and will come from the twenty-two letters.

Contemplative and chanting exercises require each *Sephirah* to have its own God-name; unfortunately, this Verse provides only eight names. Glotzer, Kaplan and Stenring provide ten names in their commentaries, and Israel Regardie's *The Middle Pillar* gives us the ten names most often used by today's occult organizations. Table 7, **Sephirotic God-Names** compares these different lists of ten Names of God. Glotzer's list unfortunately has Hod and Netzach sharing the name *Tzvaot*; Kaplan's list is unsatisfactory in that it uses the pronunciation of *Elohim* for both *Binah* and *Gevurah*. The lists given by Stenring and Regardie are preferred by most students for the simple reason that they avoid duplication. Students today use a variety of God-names for the *Sephirot*, and there is no accepted standard.

Suggestions for working with this Verse:

1. Using the ten God-names given by Stenring, envision the *Sephirot* as shown in Figure 18, **Stenring's Godnames on the Tree**, and chant the names in order: *Aleph-Hey-Yud-Hey, Yah, Yod Heh Vav Heh, Elohim, Elohim Yod Heh Vav Heh, Yod Heh Vav Heh Tzvaot, Elohim Tzabaoth, Al, Shaddai, Yod Heh Vav Heh Adonoy.*

Table 7: Sephirotic God-names

Sephirah	Glotzer	Kaplan	Stenring	Regardie
Keter	Aleph Heh Yud Heh (EhHeh Yeh)	Ehyeh	Aleph Heh Yud Heh	Eheieh
Chokmah	Yud-Hey (Yah)	Yah	Yud Hey (Yah)	Yhvh Elohim
Binah	Yud-Hey-Vav-Hey Elohim	YHVH (Elohim)	Yud Hey Vav Heh	Yhvh Elohim
Chesed	El	El	Elohim	El
Gevurah	Elohim	Elohim	Elohim Yud Hey Vav Hey	Elohim Gibor
Tifaret	Yud-Hey-Vav-Hey	YHVH	Yud Hey Vav Hey Tzabaoth	Yhvh Eloah ve-Daath
Netzach	Tzvaot (shared with Hod)	YHVH Tzavoat	Elohim Tzabaoth	Yhvh Tzabaoth
Hod	Tzvaot (shared with Netzach)	Elohim Tzavaot	Al	Elohim Tzabaoth
Yesod	Shaddai	El Shaddai	Shaddai	Shaddai El Chai
Makluth	Aleph-Dalet-Nun-Yud (Adonoi)	YHVH Adonoy	YHVH Adonoy	Adonai ha-Aretz

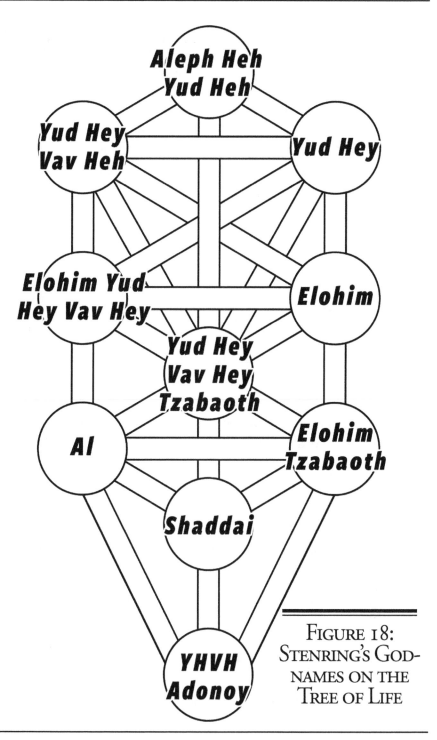

FIGURE 18:
STENRING'S GOD-
NAMES ON THE
TREE OF LIFE

Verse 6:7 The Covenant

When Abraham, may he rest in peace, observed, looked, saw, investigated, understood, engraved, hewed, combined, formed and succeeded, then the Master of All, blessed be He, revealed Himself to him. He sat him in His lap and kissed him on his head and called him friend. He made with him a covenant between the ten toes of his feet, the covenant of circumcision, and a covenant between the ten fingers of his hands, which is the covenant of the tongue. He bound the twenty-two letters into his tongue and revealed to him their foundation. He soaked them in water, He burnt them in fire, He agitated them in the wind, He illuminated them in the seven planets and directed them with the twelve constellations.

It is as a result of this Verse that the *Sefer Yetzirah* is attributed to Abraham. It may be argued that Abraham would not have written about himself in the third person. The same difficulty exists with respect to the Torah, which is believed to have been written by Moses, but contains an account of Moses' death. (Glotzer quotes Rabbi Meir as saying that Moses did indeed write those last few lines, which were dictated to him by God.[57]) It may be that Abraham wrote about himself in the 3rd person; it may be that Rabbi Akiva added this last Verse to the *Sefer Yetzirah*; or it may be that the *Sefer Yetzirah* was written by someone else entirely.

The various activities attributed to Abraham (observing, looking, seeing, investigating, understanding, hewing, combining, forming and succeeding) are believed by some to mean that Abraham made golems; but it is more likely that these words refer to spiritual techniques. As a result of Abraham's success in these endeavors, God revealed Himself to Abraham. God made two covenants with Abraham: the covenant of circumcision and the covenant of the tongue.

As we saw in Chapter One, the covenant of the tongue may refer to

---

57 Glotzer, Leonard R. *The Fundamentals of Jewish Mysticism: The Book of Creation and Its Commentaries.* Northvale, NJ: Jason Aronson, Inc., 1992, p. 207.

Torah, though this seems unlikely since the Torah won't be given to the People for another 300 years or so after Abraham. It is more likely that the covenant of the tongue refers to the ability to create with language, particularly as most translations state that the twenty-two letters were tied or bound into Abraham's tongue.

The emphasis on the tongue here (as well as in Verses 1:3, 2:1 and 3:1) leads us to suspect that creation with the twenty-two letters requires us to actually speak the letters, not merely meditate upon them. The word "tongue" is also used in the *Sefer Yetzirah* to denote balance; both our words and our sexuality must be kept in balance for the power of the letters to become manifest.

Thus, the two covenants are ways in which we are raised by God above the animals. Sexuality symbolizes the "animal" part of human nature; through the covenant of circumcision, we agree to be more than animal. As a result, we are invited to engage in the second covenant, the covenant of the tongue, which gives us the power to create.

God's activity with respect to the 22 letters is summarized in this Verse. He subjected them to the Law of Three (the elements of water, wind and fire), the Law of Seven (the planets) and the Law of Twelve (the constellations).

The complete assignment of Hebrew letters to paths is shown in Figure 19, **22 Letters on the Tree**. Writing, contemplating and chanting the Hebrew letters allows the student to navigate the paths of the Tree in his consciousness. Also see Figure 20, **Letters on the Tree According to the Tarot Tradition**.

Suggestions for working with this Verse:

1. Consider the ways in which we humans strive to be more than animals. Are we successful?

2. Does the power of speech endow us with the power of creation? How might we use it more wisely?

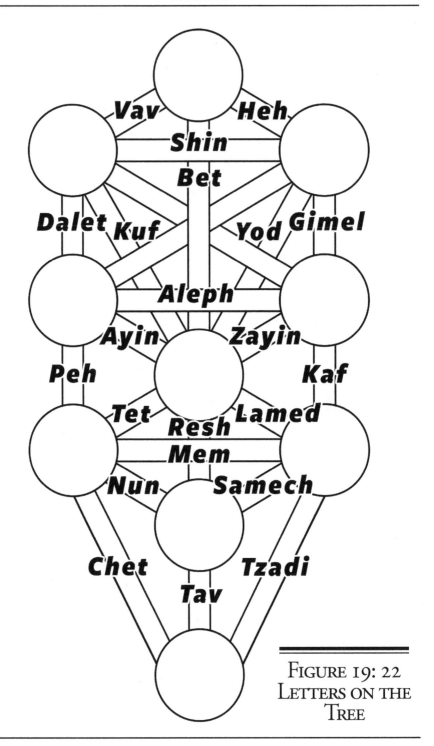

FIGURE 19: 22
LETTERS ON THE
TREE

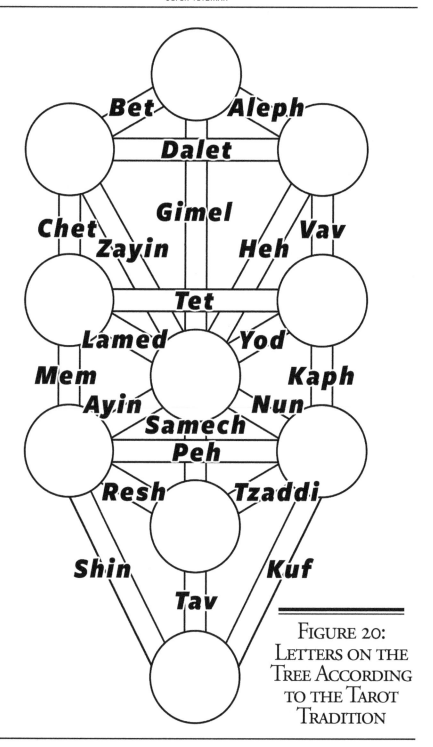

FIGURE 20:
LETTERS ON THE
TREE ACCORDING
TO THE TAROT
TRADITION

CPSIA information can be obtained
at www.ICGtesting.com
Printed in the USA
LVHW08s1611041018
592106LV00026B/629/P